Bankruptcy for Small Business

WENDELL SCHOLLANDER
WES SCHOLLANDER
Attorneys at Law

**Vincennes University
Shake Learning Resources Center
Vincennes, In 47591-9986**

SPHINX® PUBLISHING
AN IMPRINT OF SOURCEBOOKS, INC.®
NAPERVILLE, ILLINOIS
www.SphinxLegal.com

First Edition: 2008

Published by: **Sphinx® Publishing, An Imprint of Sourcebooks, Inc.®**

Naperville Office
P.O. Box 4410
Naperville, Illinois 60567-4410
630-961-3900
Fax: 630-961-2168
www.sourcebooks.com
www.SphinxLegal.com

This publication is designed to provide accurate and authoritative information in regard to the subject matter covered. It is sold with the understanding that the publisher is not engaged in rendering legal, accounting, or other professional service. If legal advice or other expert assistance is required, the services of a competent professional person should be sought.

From a Declaration of Principles Jointly Adopted by a Committee of the American Bar Association and a Committee of Publishers and Associations

This product is not a substitute for legal advice.

Disclaimer required by Texas statutes.

Library of Congress Cataloging-in-Publication Data

Schollander, Wendell
  Bankruptcy for small business / by Wendell Schollander and Wes Schollander. — 1st ed.
      p. cm.
  Includes index.
   ISBN 978-1-57248-665-2 (pbk. : alk. paper) 1. Bankruptcy—United States—Popular works. 2. Small business—Law and legislation—United States—Popular works.   I. Schollander, Wes, 1974- II. Title.
   KF1524.85.S36 2008
   346.7307'8—dc22

                              2008016283

CONTENTS

USING SELF-HELP LAW BOOKS

Before using a self-help law book, you should realize the advantages and disadvantages of doing your own legal work and understand the challenges and diligence that this requires.

The Growing Trend

Rest assured that you will not be the first or only person handling your own legal matter. For example, in some states, more than 75% of the people in divorces and other cases represent themselves. Because of the high cost of legal services, this is a major trend, and many courts are struggling to make it easier for people to represent themselves. However, some courts are not happy with people who do not use attorneys and refuse to help them in any way. For some, the attitude is, "Go to the law library and figure it out for yourself."

We write and publish self-help law books to give people an alternative to the often complicated and confusing legal books found in most law libraries. We have made the explanations of the law as simple and easy to understand as possible. Of course, unlike an attorney advising an individual client, we cannot cover every conceivable possibility.

Cost/Value Analysis

Whenever you shop for a product or service, you are faced with various levels of quality and price. In deciding what product or service to buy, you make a cost/value analysis on the basis of your willingness to pay and the quality you desire.

When buying a car, you decide whether you want transportation, comfort, status, or sex appeal. Accordingly, you decide among choices such as a Neon, a Lincoln, a Rolls Royce, or a Porsche. Before making a decision, you usually weigh the merits of each option against the cost.

When you get a headache, you can take a pain reliever (such as aspirin) or visit a medical specialist for a neurological examination. Given this choice, most people, of course, take a pain reliever, since it costs only pennies; whereas a medical examination costs hundreds of dollars and takes a lot of time. This is usually a logical choice because it is rare to need anything more than a pain reliever for a headache. But in some cases, a headache may indicate a brain tumor, and failing to see a specialist right away can result in complications. Should everyone with a headache go to a specialist? Of course not, but people treating their own illnesses must realize that they are betting, on the basis of their cost/value analysis of the situation, that they are taking the most logical option.

The same cost/value analysis must be made when deciding to do one's own legal work. Many legal situations are very straightforward, requiring a simple form and no complicated analysis. Anyone with a little intelligence and a book of instructions can handle the matter without outside help.

But there is always the chance that complications are involved that only an attorney would notice. To simplify the law into a book like this, several legal cases often must be condensed into a single sentence or paragraph. Otherwise, the book would be several hundred pages long and too complicated for most people. However, this simplification necessarily leaves out many details and nuances that would apply to special or unusual situations. Also, there are many ways to interpret most legal questions. Your case may come before a judge who disagrees with the analysis of our authors.

Therefore, in deciding to use a self-help law book and to do your own legal work, you must realize that you are making a cost/value analysis. You have decided that the money you will save in doing it yourself outweighs the chance that your case will not turn out to your satisfaction. Most people handling their own simple legal matters never have a problem, but occasionally people find that it ended up costing them more to have an attorney straighten out the situation than it would have if they had hired an attorney in the beginning. Keep this in mind while handling your case, and be sure to consult an attorney if you feel you might need further guidance.

Local Rules

The next thing to remember is that a book which covers the law for the entire nation, or even for an entire state, cannot possibly include every procedural difference of every jurisdiction. Whenever possible, we provide the exact form needed; however, in some areas, each county, or even each judge, may require unique forms and procedures. In our state books, our forms usually cover the majority of counties in the state or provide examples of the type of form that will be required. In our national books, our forms are sometimes even more general in nature but are designed to give a good idea of the type of form that will be needed in most locations. Nonetheless, keep in mind that your state, county, or judge may have a requirement, or use a form, that is not included in this book.

You should not necessarily expect to be able to get all of the information and resources you need solely from within the pages of this book. This book will serve as your guide, giving you specific information whenever possible and helping you to find out what else you will need to know. This is just like if you decided to build your own backyard deck. You might purchase a book on how to build decks. However, such a book would not include the building codes and permit requirements of every city, town, county, and township in the nation; nor would it include the lumber, nails, saws, hammers, and other materials and tools you would need to actually build the deck. You would use the book as your guide, and then do some work and research involving such matters as whether you need a permit of some kind, what type and grade of wood is available in your area, whether to use hand tools or power tools, and how to use those tools.

Before using the forms in a book like this, you should check with your court clerk to see if there are any local rules of which you should be aware or local forms you will need to use. Often, such forms will require the same information as the forms in the book but are merely laid out differently or use slightly different language. They will sometimes require additional information.

Changes in the Law

Besides being subject to local rules and practices, the law is subject to change at any time. The courts and the legislatures of all fifty states are constantly revising the laws. It is possible that while you are reading this book, some aspect of the law is being changed.

In most cases, the change will be of minimal significance. A form will be redesigned, additional information will be required, or a waiting period will be extended. As a result, you might need to revise a form, file an extra form, or wait out a longer time period. These types of changes will not usually affect the outcome of your case. On the other hand, sometimes a major part of the law is changed, the entire law in a particular area is rewritten, or a case that was the basis of a central legal point is overruled. In such instances, your entire ability to pursue your case may be impaired.

INTRODUCTION

The small business owner faces a host of problems and challenges in operating a business. The bookshelves are full of books with advice on how to succeed and how to make money. However, there is almost nothing that gives guidance to the owners of the eight out of ten small businesses that run into financial problems.

We are bankruptcy lawyers and have long been frustrated by the mistakes people make when they face money problems. Often these mistakes are made out of a lack of knowledge about the insolvency process and the fear of what can happen. This book will try to help people avoid these mistakes, and it endeavors to remove some of the fear by explaining how the system works.

By necessity, legal principles will be covered throughout this book. Learning about legal issues is not easy. It is often said that the law is a *seamless web*. What is meant by that is when you are learning about one area of law, you are likely to need a prior understanding of several other areas of law to understand the new topic. The problem, of course, is that when you are starting your study, you do not know about the other areas. If you decide to learn more about those other areas, they in turn will depend on a prior knowledge of even still different legal areas.

Thus in writing about bankruptcy for small businesses, we will often need to cover some of the same information in several different places in this book. This way you will not have to learn as much extraneous law as you otherwise would need to.

In our practice we see many small business owners who, by the time they come to us, have taken steps that prevent them from using the bankruptcy laws to save their businesses, homes, or other property. It is our goal in writing this book to provide you with the information necessary to avoid these mistakes, as well as a full overview of how to navigate your business from the first hint of money problems through bankruptcy and on to financial recovery.

The organization of this work reflects the journey most people take as they face money problems and contemplate bankruptcy. The beginning sections deal with the information gathering and review stages. Section 1 explains business organization, Section 2 reveals why small business owners are more likely to face financial problems, Section 3 describes what bill collectors can and cannot do, Section 4 discusses the different types of bankruptcy that may be available to you, Section 5 concerns how a business owner's personal and business financial life intermix, Section 6 lists myths about debt and bankruptcy, Section 7 provides alternatives to bankruptcy, Section 8 talks about what lawyers can do to help, Section 9 reveals common mistakes people make when they have money problems, Section 10 highlights the importance of making a financial analysis of your business's status, Section 11 teaches how to take a personal financial inventory, Section 12 identifies what property you may lose if you file bankruptcy, and Section 13 explains steps to take (and avoid) prior to filing for bankruptcy.

The book then moves on to examine the bankruptcy process itself—Chapters 7, 11, and 13 bankruptcies, and the issues that can come up after you file for bankruptcy (Sections 14 through 17).

The final sections cover life after bankruptcy, including continuing your business (Section 18) and rebuilding your credit (Section 19).

This book is designed to be read a bit at a time, rather than straight through in one sitting. You should allow yourself time to read through it slowly so you can make sure you fully understand the bankruptcy process. Depending on where you are in your financial journey, you may wish to first read about the myths of debt and bankruptcy, or what mistakes to avoid in operating your business in bad times. We hope you will find the information and approach helpful.

Types of Small Businesses and Their Operations

There are many different ways to organize a business—from sole proprietorships to subchapter S corporations. Over the years we have found that many small business owners do not know what type of business organization they are operating under. Often they think their business is a corporation because they use the word *company* in the business's name. Sometimes they know a lawyer or accountant took care of the legal formalities when the business was formed years ago, but they do not know exactly what was done and have not worried about it since.

Since the nature of a business can have a great effect on what type of bankruptcy you or the company can file, it is worthwhile to take a minute to read over this section.

Sole Proprietorships

The most common business form in the United States is the *sole proprietorship*. All forms of business, from the corner lemonade stand to multimillion dollar companies, can exist as sole proprietorships. Unlike a corporation or a limited liability company (LLC), nothing needs to be filed with the government in order to bring a sole proprietorship into existence. A sole proprietorship is formed the instant a person begins operating a business without a partner or filing to change the business's status.

A *sole proprietorship* is the legal term for an individual operating a business without special status (such as corporate status). A sole proprietorship is merely an extension of the person who is operating the business. The business's debts are considered to be personal debts of the entrepreneur while the business's assets can be reached in order to satisfy the individual's personal debts. There is no legal distinction between the person and the business.

The most prevalent misconception surrounding sole proprietorships is that once the business's assets are sold off, the business's creditors cannot go after the individual's property. This is wrong. Because the sole proprietorship and the entrepreneur are considered one and the same, a debt against one is treated as a debt against the other. The entrepreneur must incorporate or seek some other form of legal protection in order to protect his or her personal property.

Partnerships

A *partnership* is formed when two or more individuals agree to operate a business without filing for special status. Partnerships are very easy to form. A partnership is usually formed once an agreement is made about how to split profits. This agreement can be written or oral.

Once a partnership is formed, all partners are personally responsible for all the business's debts. A creditor can usually sue a partner for the full amount of a debt once the partnership's assets have been exhausted. A partnership offers no protection to its members' assets. Much like a sole proprietorship, a partnership is simply an extension of its members' estates. It is not a separate legal entity.

The great danger in a partnership is that one partner can create a debt that holds the other partner or partners accountable even if the others did not know about the debt in the first place.

Corporations

Corporations are the most common form of special legal business status in the United States. Filing for corporate status shields shareholders from liability on corporate debts. The *corporation* is treated like a separate entity that is responsible for its own debts. Once the corporation's assets are exhausted, barring any agreements to the contrary, creditors have no further recourse against the shareholders.

Filing for corporate status is a relatively simple procedure. A lawyer can help you legally incorporate your business and follow your state's guidelines as to how to maintain corporate status. Every state requires a corporation to meet minimal operational guidelines such as maintaining corporate procedures (i.e., electing a board of directors and holding corporate meetings) and avoiding commingling of corporate and individual assets. Failure to follow these corporate formalities results in the loss of the *corporate shield*. Although not overly complicated, corporate formalities are required in order to maintain the corporate shield and provide protection for the shareholders.

The small business owner, however, faces an even greater hurdle to preserving corporate protection than just following proper corporate procedures. Creditors know that once a corporation's assets are dissolved, barring any further agreements, they will be unable to get at the entrepreneur's personal assets. Since most small business corporations have no assets, creditors will want to have another way to protect themselves financially. This means that creditors will almost always require the entrepreneur to personally guarantee the debt. In this way, if the corporation fails and lacks the assets to fully pay all of its debts, creditors can then go after the individual behind the corporation.

Be careful when signing contracts on a corporation's behalf. Most small business contracts are written by creditors who have lawyers working for them. Contracts are almost always written in a way that if the corporation fails, the entrepreneur is then personally liable. Unless you sign the contract "John Doe, on behalf of Corporation, Inc." or something similar, you are more than likely also personally liable for the debt. It is very common for small business owners to insist that it is only the corporation that is liable on a debt and not them personally, and then come to find out once they actually read the contract that they are in fact personally liable.

Some people believe that forming an *S corporation* will provide further protection as to corporate debt or obligations as a grantor. This is not true. The *S corporation* is merely a tax device to modify income tax payments; it has no effect on corporate debts.

In theory, a corporation is a good means for a business owner to protect his or her personal property from liability on business debts. In reality, a small business owner will have problems maintaining corporate protection. Even if all corporate formalities are followed, creditors are loath to lend money to a small corporation without a personal guarantee on the loan.

Limited Liability Companies

Not too long ago, *limited liability companies* (LLCs) did not exist. However, by 1997, every state in the country had formally recognized such business entities. The rapid growth in LLCs' popularity is due to the fact that LLCs offer the same protection as corporations, but there is no double-taxation problem. An LLC is treated the same as a sole proprietorship or partnership for tax purposes while providing an individual with a corporate shield.

The small business entrepreneur, however, must still be careful to limit his or her personal liability when signing contracts. Some states may also require certain formalities for LLCs, although there tend to be fewer formalities for LLCs than for corporations. LLCs fill a void in U.S. business structures, giving the security of the corporate shield without the problems of double taxation or corporate formalities. A local attorney should be able to explain your state's LLC requirements and help you comply with them.

THE SPECIAL CHALLENGES OF BEING AN ENTREPRENEUR

2

This book is for small business owners and entrepreneurs who are facing money problems and considering filing for bankruptcy. Small business owners include anyone who owns a business in which he or she is a key element. People who have a skill they sell (such as carpenters, doctors, interpreters, or art directors), people who sell a service (such as lawn mowing services, truckers, or funeral home directors), and those who sell products (such as builders, merchants, or small manufacturers) are in this group.

As you read through this book you will find as many references to personal finances as you will to business finances. This is because for most small business owners, the two are intertwined. Often, entrepreneurs personally guarantee business loans. They use credit cards and personal loans to tide them over when the business is not producing sufficient income for them to live on. Many times they personally own the vehicles and equipment the business is using, or their personal car is owned by the small business. For this reason, any time a small business owner is forced to consider business bankruptcy, his or her personal financial status must be examined along with the business's finances.

Double-Sided Pressure

The small business owner is often under pressure on two fronts. First, the business operation can come across a host of possible problems, including the normal problems that can affect anyone—illness, injury, and family problems. When times turn bad, the business encounters the second front—collection calls and lawsuits by business creditors as well as personal creditors. To this must be added fears about the future of a business owner's livelihood. The pressure can be overwhelming, and the worst part is that the business owner is often facing this pressure alone.

Reasons for Money Problems

After interviewing thousands of business owners who are experiencing debt problems or money stress, we discovered that they almost inevitably experience those money problems because:

- customers run into their own cash flow problems or just will not pay;

- a business recession or other change in the general economic climate causes a drop in orders;

- new competitors are keeping prices down; or,

- costs have increased more than prices can be raised.

None of these problems are caused by the business owner. They are the product of a dog-eat-dog business system.

To these business problems must be added the problems a person can have in his or her personal life. He or she can have a relationship end and be stuck with bills for two, or experience medical debt often combined with an income loss because of the illness or injury, for example.

Because the small business owner often finds his or her personal and business lives intertwined, debts for one often serve as funds for the other. For this reason, trends in personal finance are very important for the business owner.

Another problem is that incomes for the average person (including the business owner) are not rising as fast as the cost of living. Over the last fifteen or twenty years, the average person has lost ground financially. This has two effects. First, small business owners often operate close to the edge in terms of finances with little room for error. Second, they increase their debt as they try to maintain their businesses and their standard of living. This larger debt overhang in turn makes them more vulnerable to medical emergencies, loss of income, personal tragedies, divorce, or separation.

Debt More Specifically

Debt is more deadly now than it was in the past. Interest rates are much higher than they were fifty years ago. In the late 1970s, credit card issuers and other creditors were able to increase the interest rates of their cards and loans. Court interpretations of banking laws allowed financial institutions to place credit card operations in states that permitted high interest rate charges and to sell the cards into states that tried to enforce the traditionally lower interest rates. In time, other states increased their maximum interest charges in an effort to retain or attract credit card operations and keep their lenders competitive.

The reason high interest rates were traditionally not allowed prior to the late 1970s was that everyone knew that once a person or business got behind on an 18% interest rate, or even on a 12% interest rate, it was nearly impossible to get caught up. In fact, it is very difficult to ever pay off a debt at a 12% to 18% interest rate because most of the payments are going directly to paying the interest on the debt instead of paying off the principal. If you make the minimum payments on a debt with an 18% interest rate, it will take you over fourteen years to finish paying off the debt.

Downward Spiral

One of the problems with having a financial crisis is there is really very little one can do about it over the short run. If business slows down or a person gets sick and cannot work for a month or two, there is little adjustment that can be made to his or her fixed overhead cost of living. Things such as rent, equipment leases, vehicle payments, and mortgages are fixed. The only places one can cut back are on food, entertainment, and perhaps clothing. Without an emergency reserve, if there is not enough flexibility in those three areas, a person must cut back on what is sent to creditors and suppliers each month. This leads to a vicious downward spiral that can potentially result in having to file for bankruptcy.

Creditors will charge late fees and the interest rates will keep compounding as they charge interest on the interest that accumulated from the months before. Quite often before a person knows it, he or she is deeply in debt. What then typically follows is a desperate struggle to keep the creditors at bay. This is typically referred to as *robbing Peter to pay Paul* (paying one creditor one month and then skipping a month while another creditor is paid, dodging phone calls, and getting cash advances to pay creditors). All of this puts the person and the business deeper and deeper into debt.

Generally, people want very badly to pay their debts. That is the way they were brought up and they believe it is the right thing to do. They also do not like the feeling of paying their bills in an untimely, inefficient way. Not being able to pay the obligations creates feelings of guilt and failure and the collection calls and letters add stress. This creates a typical pattern of psychological and physical stress that will be covered in the next section.

Effects of Financial Pressure

People we have interviewed reported a typical pattern of problems and symptoms when under financial pressure, including:

- insomnia;

- sickness and accidents;

- fights with a spouse or partner;

- problems at work;

- headaches;

- avoidance;

- depression; and,

- grief.

Perhaps you recognize yourself in this picture. People often do not realize how much pressure they are under because of debt stress until it is released. The pressure builds up slowly and they adjust to it each time another bill or past due notice arrives. But it is definitely still there.

They often say things such as, "I'm 40 years old, and I've worked hard all my life. I never thought I would be in a position where I was not able to pay my debts," or, "I live in a nice neighborhood and all my neighbors think I have an ideal life. I never thought this would be happening to me. No one knows what I'm going through. I don't know what I'm going to do."

Veterans of the Vietnam and the Persian Gulf Wars often say that this kind of financial pressure is worse than being in combat: "I told myself that if I lived through this war nothing would ever bother me again—but this is worse than the fear of being killed." In fact, some in a debt crisis want to die. Many debtors report that they have thoughts about suicide.

One very common concern is feeling guilty and ashamed. People do not want others to know. They do not want their parents or children to find out they have money problems, and they certainly do not want their neighbors and coworkers to find out. The effect of this is to isolate the individual and to prevent the stress from being released in a healthy way.

People having this kind of financial trouble do not realize how many other people have the same problem. There are thousands of cases each year moving through the bankruptcy court, and many more cases being dealt with through consumer credit counseling and other businesses handling debt problems. It is rare for a business to not have money problems at some point. But debt problems are largely a hidden epidemic. Since everyone is hiding their problem, everyone thinks they are the only one having such problems. These debt problems cut across all financial strata. We have had many clients come to us who had been making $100,000 or more a year and still almost had their homes foreclosed because they were in so much financial trouble.

One answer to avoiding financial problems that arise from a reduction in income or unexpected medical expenses is to have an emergency fund set aside. Experts recommend a reserve of ready money equal to six to ten months of income. While this is good advice, in practice almost no one can follow it. High tax rates make it hard to earn enough money to merely keep a business going and to raise a family, let alone bank six to ten months of salary.

The entrepreneur's natural instinct is to invest profits back into the business to make it grow. Trying to save a half-year's income from after-tax money is very hard, financially and psychologically. And even if you do manage to save this month, where do you keep it? Most people tend to invest these funds in stocks. When a recession hits, they often get a double blow—they lose their job and the value of their emergency fund drops.

The Dangers of Past-Due Debts, Bankruptcy, and the Collection Process

3

Because they are under pressure from two sides, small business owners must worry about the action of both business and personal creditors. People collecting for creditors will often threaten or seem to threaten all types of dire actions—some of which they cannot legally do. It is good to have an idea of what can, and more importantly, cannot be done to you by your creditors.

Business Creditors

A creditor who has a claim against a business alone has a limited number of options. A creditor can and will, as a first measure, cut off future credit and sales. Creditors who have interest in equipment and inventory may try to have the property turned over to them voluntarily, often with the threat of a lawsuit if the equipment and inventory is not turned over to them. In some cases, equipment may be seized. It is fairly unusual for a large business creditor to call you at home or contact family members or coworkers, but it does happen in some cases. Banks may *accelerate* (ask for full payment) loans and *freeze* (prohibit any withdrawal) money held in your account to cover debts owed to them.

Personal Creditors

In the great majority of cases where there is a money problem with a small business, the problem transforms itself into personal debt and the entrepreneur must deal with personal creditors. There are two reasons for this. First, most banks or businesses will not loan money, lease equipment, or rent space to a business without *personal guarantees* (a guarantee in a person's name rather than in the business's name). Second, the business owner often uses his or her personal credit to obtain funds for the business or to operate the business. We have all heard of the film producer who made a movie using cash advances from credit cards, or the business owner who lived on credit cards while waiting for his or her business to get off the ground or during a slow period for the business.

It is normally the *personal debts* the small business has accrued that drive the owner to see a lawyer, as these tend to be the ones that put a great deal of the stress on the individual. Quite often, business owners turn to credit cards or personal loans from finance companies to bridge shortfalls in business income. In addition, they offer up their homes and personal vehicles as collateral for loans taken out to fund the business.

Steps the Creditor Cannot Take

Owing money you cannot pay is stressful partly because you feel guilty and maybe like a failure. The other source of stress is from bill collectors and their tactics. When you start receiving phone calls from collections people, they are often quite aggressive, if not abusive. We have been told many times that creditors threaten to have the debtor arrested and put in jail, or to have his or her salary or tax refund garnished. Creditors often tell people that it is fraud to not pay back the money they borrowed.

Jail

One cannot be arrested and put in jail for a civil debt owed to a credit card company or a bank. Normally, the only time you can be sent to jail is when you break a law or fail to obey an order of the court in a family matter. Owing money to a person is not a crime and is not something for which you can be jailed. The United States has done away with debtors' prison. Nowhere in the United States can a creditor seize your paycheck or property without a lawsuit and the opportunity for you to have a trial.

Seizing Property

Creditors will sometimes say things such as, "We are going to take all of your property," or if they are particularly sadistic, "We are going to take your kids' furniture and pets." People have visions of their things being taken from their homes and piled up in their front yards for everyone to see. This is almost certain to never happen, so try not to let this threat bother you. A creditor cannot just call a police officer and start hauling furniture out of your house. Even if a creditor wanted your furniture, he or she would have to get a court order before invading your home or office. This means that your creditor would have to go to the expense of a lawsuit.

Tax Refunds

A private company cannot have the government seize your tax refund. If you owe taxes or money on a government-guaranteed student loan, then you can have your tax refund seized by the government, but a private company does not have this authority. If someone who is not part of a government entity or collecting for a government entity threatens to seize your tax refund, take this threat with a very large grain of salt.

Wage Garnishment

It is quite common for creditors to threaten to have your wages *garnished* (money removed from your paycheck to send directly to the creditors). This is a powerful collection tool if you are earning a wage, but of limited use against a self-employed individual. Additionally, not every state allows wage garnishment.

Harassment

Given the limited range of what credit collectors can do without filing a lawsuit, they often start by pestering or harassing you to distraction. We have had reports of people getting calls from the same creditor several times a day. Calls start at seven o'clock in the morning and go to eleven o'clock at night. Collectors often call debtors at work after being asked not to, and many times the receptionist or other employees are told about the person's financial problems. Family members are often called and told about the person's debt problems. We have even had cases where collection people talked to neighbors and told them the person was not paying his or her bills.

Books on debt management often advise readers who are having extensive financial problems to contact their creditors, explain the situation to them, and try to work out a reduced payment schedule. In our experience, this almost never works. It may be possible to work out something with one creditor, but if there are several creditors, there are almost always some who will not work with you and insist on full payment. Some will insult you as you pour your heart out to them. Unless all creditors agree to a reduced payment, it is unlikely that setting up a system of reduced payments will work to solve your financial problems.

The other problem with this advice is that you often talk to a different person every time you call the creditor or the collection agency. You can make an agreement with one person at the agency, and then a few days later get an abusive collection call from someone else at the same company. When you try to explain to the new person that you have worked out a reduced payment plan with someone else at the company, he or she often will deny any knowledge of it and demand full payment at once. Often he or she will say, "I have never heard of that person," or, "There is no such arrangement noted in the computer." It is emotionally exhausting trying to explain the same thing over and over again every few days while being verbally abused.

We have heard this sequence of events told to us so often that we are convinced the collectors are using one or two techniques. One is *good cop/bad cop*, where one collector will be nice and understanding and the next will be hateful and try to break you down. The other is the *wolf pack method*. When wolves hunt a deer, one does not run up and kill the deer. Rather, they will take turns running up to the animal and biting a bit of flesh away. No one bite kills the deer. The deer bleeds to death or just gives up in exhaustion.

Laws against harassment. People who are subject to harassing collection actions often ask whether there are laws against what their creditors are doing—calling three to four times a day plus calling coworkers, family members, and neighbors. There are federal laws, and many states have laws against unfair collections tactics.

The *Fair Debt Collection Practices Act of 1978* (FDCPA) bars all of these acts and regulates the activities of debt collectors. The law prohibits almost all collector contacts with family, except spouses. It bars contact with neighbors, except to learn the consumer's address and phone number or work address. However, if the creditor contacts a neighbor, he or she is not allowed to tell the neighbor that the person owes money or volunteer the collection company's name.

The collector also may not contact the consumer at inconvenient times—before 8:00 a.m. and after 9:00 p.m.—or at inconvenient places. He or she may not make burdensome, repetitive phone calls or use obscene or abusive language. A person's place of employment is considered an inconvenient place unless there is no other way to reach the consumer. The collector cannot threaten to file a lawsuit when there is no intent to actually do so. He or she cannot take any other actions that would serve to harass, oppress, or abuse the consumer. Debt collectors also cannot continue to contact you after being told that you are represented by an attorney.

The FDCPA states that the consumer may write the debt collector or creditor to say that he or she refuses to pay the debt or wishes to have all further communications cease. If this is done, the only communication the debt collector or creditor can have with the consumer is to:

- advise the consumer that debt collection efforts are being terminated;

- notify the consumer that specified *remedies* (lawsuits) may be invoked; and,

- notify the consumer that the debt collector or creditor intends to invoke a specified remedy.

Law is of limited help. While the FDCPA bars almost all the collection actions that bother people with money problems, its enforcement provisions offer little assistance when creditors violate the law. If an individual files a lawsuit, the damages that can actually be collected are small, and proving the case is rather difficult. For these reasons, lawyers are reluctant to bring individual suits for violations of the FDCPA. Almost all cases brought under this law are *class action lawsuits* (groups of people with a similar legal case against the same party), and an individual's odds of having his or her creditor's violations turned into a class action lawsuit are small.

Consumer protection agencies. What about the consumer protection agencies? Government agencies and consumer protection lawyers are set up to deal with class action lawsuits rather than help individuals.

Basically, you are on your own in pursuing a legal case against your creditors, and as a practical matter the creditors can do just about anything they want. There are only two avenues to get help. One is Consumer Credit Counseling and the other is a private debt manager who, if you can pay enough, may be able to set up a payment program that will satisfy all of your creditors. These options will be covered in detail in Section 7.

Steps the Creditor Can Take

One of the first things business suppliers do when you stop paying them is to stop supplying products, or put you on *cash on delivery* (COD), which can badly hamper businesses that depend on credit from suppliers. However, there are many businesses not affected by this type of pressure, such as freight haulers, doctors, lawyers, carpenters, service providers, etc. Their normal mode of operation is to pay for supplies at the time they receive them. If these types of businesses have outstanding debt not being paid, then reasonable phone calls from lenders or suppliers who need their money to stay in business are allowed.

Lawsuit

When creditors give up on calling you, the next step is a lawsuit. Suing you is not an abusive collection method. You owe the money to the creditor, and the creditor has the right to go to court to try to collect it from you.

People are often thrown into a panic when they first hear about a lawsuit. Some creditors will describe a lawsuit in such a way as to make people think they will be put in jail. They will say things like, "I'll send the sheriff out with papers."

As noted earlier, you cannot be put in jail for a civil debt. The normal way to serve lawsuit papers is to have a sheriff or other process server deliver them. Sometimes they are simply mailed to you, but many states require notice of a lawsuit to be *personally served* (given to the person being sued in person). Service by sheriff is a favored threat of creditors since it upsets people, and people fear the vision of having a law officer come to where they work or live and serve papers on them in front of their coworkers or neighbors.

When the papers are served, they often say that you must answer within so many days, usually thirty. You will not get arrested if you do not give the court an answer or go to court. It is only criminal court where you can be arrested for not appearing in court. Debt collection lawsuits are civil suits. However, if you are not there to argue your case and the other side can show you owe them the money they say you do, the court will usually issue a judgment against you. So, while you are not required to go to court, it is not a bad idea to check with a lawyer to see if you have any defenses against the lawsuit. At the same time, you can get detailed information on what collection actions the creditor can legally take against you after it has obtained its court judgment. The following is a general overview of collection actions that can occur.

Judgment against you. A judgment against you may have very little effect, or it can be a disaster. The collection process after a lawsuit or foreclosure hearing is the danger point for any debtor.

Creditors are allowed to take certain steps to collect a judgment, and now they have a court order on their side. In cases of secured property, the court will direct that the property be turned over to the creditor, if the creditor has not been able to pick it up on its own.

Seizing property and the exemption form. Another step is to have a sheriff take the debtors' other property to collect the judgment. Normally this involves first sending notice to the debtors that they have the right to protect certain assets if they are listed on a form turned in to the court within a limited number of days. Since the form is often a bit complicated, and since ignoring the creditor has worked in the past, some people do not fill out the form. This is a serious mistake. If the form is not filled out, the creditor can seize any property the debtor owns, often including his or her home. A favorite target when the debtor does not fill out this exemption form is the debtor's car. This puts maximum pressure on the debtor as he or she usually needs the car to get to work, and there is a ready market for used cars.

The form normally has different types of property that can be protected. Depending on the state, this protected property area may be sufficiently generous that the creditor cannot seize any property. Should this be the case the debtor is said to be *judgment proof*.

If your property in a given category is worth more than can be protected, which is often the case for business owners, the creditor can send a sheriff out to pick it up and sell it. At these sales, the property is often sold for far less than it is actually worth. This amount is subtracted from the amount owed and the debtor is still responsible for the remaining debt.

Judgment lien. There is another way a judgment can harm a debtor. The judgment becomes a *judgment lien* against land and homes, which means that when the property is sold, the money owed must be paid to the creditor. Land, other than a person's home, can often be taken at once. (It is harder to make a general statement about a person's home. It may be protected or not depending on the state one lives in.)

Example:

Suppose Sue owns a home worth $100,000 in a state where she can protect $10,000 of home equity. There is a judgment lien against the home for $3,000. She owes $95,000 so she only has $5,000 worth of equity ($100,000 − $95,000 = $5,000). Her home is protected.

However, if she should sell the home, the $95,000 mortgage and the judgment lien must be paid from the money she receives for the sale of her home.

Because of this fact, creditors oftentimes do not bother with trying to take personal assets, but instead merely wait for the debtor to sell his or her home. They know that almost all buyers will require any judgment lien to be paid off as part of the purchase of the land or home.

Foreclosure

Another legal process that may come into play is *foreclosure* (forced sale of a home by a lender). It is common for business owners to let home payments slide while they devote all their time and money to keeping the business going. Foreclosure is threatened more often than it is done because creditors know it will upset the home owner. Creditors do not really want your home if there is a good chance they can get the money owed them in a reasonable, timely way. Creditors, however, will often be demanding about house payments because they know they have such a powerful weapon to use against you.

The foreclosure process works as follows.

- First you are served a notice of a legal hearing. This gives you the chance to offer any legal defense you may have. Having an illness or other problems is not a legal defense. You should see a lawyer to discuss any defenses you might have in your individual case.

- Once the foreclosure hearing has been held, the property is advertised for a foreclosure sale. Since these advertisements are designed to inform as many people as possible about the availability of the property, they can be quite embarrassing.

- On the sale day, the property is auctioned off to the highest bidder. This is often done in an obscure part of the local courthouse. After the sale is done, there is often a limited amount of time for an upset bid. At the end of the process, your home is no longer yours and you must move out.

Bankruptcy is a powerful tool to stop a foreclosure. You may not qualify, but rather than lose your home, you should investigate the possibility.

Exceptions to the Need for Court Proceedings

There are two notable exceptions to creditors immediately filing a lawsuit. One is the *right of offset*. If you owe money to a bank or credit union and have money on deposit there, the bank or credit union can take enough of your money to pay off all or part of the debt. Be careful to remove any money from any financial institution that you owe money to. If you are in a financial crisis with a tight budget, it will be even tighter if the bank seizes what little money you have on hand to pay your rent or buy food.

The other exception is the *right of repossession*. A creditor who loaned you the money to buy your equipment, car, or truck can take the equipment or vehicle back if it has a *security interest* in the vehicle. (*Lessors*—those who lend property on lease—can take back leased equipment since it belongs to them. No one else can take it without a court order or permission.) If creditors have a security interest, they can take the property and sell it to recover the money you owe them. They cannot use force or violence to take the property and often must stop if you act like you will fight them for it. This is why repossessions are often done at night or while a business owner is away. Creditors are not allowed to trespass on private property to do their work, but since they often act when no one is around, some violate this rule. Once they have the vehicle, it is your word against theirs as to where the car was parked.

Once the creditor has the property, it will give you a little time to pay off the loan, and if you do not pay the entire loan amount, the property will be sold at auction. The auction sale price is almost always far less than what you owe on the property. You are responsible for the difference between what you promised to pay and what was received for it at the auction. This difference is called the *deficiency*. The debt is not extinguished merely because the creditor has the property back—you still owe the money you promised to pay them, less the bit the creditor received at the auction. This is why a voluntary surrender does not help you. You will still be responsible for the deficiency after the property is sold. Often, the fact that you voluntarily gave back the property does not even help you on your credit report. A voluntary surrender is often shown as a *repossession* on your credit report.

Overview of Bankruptcy and How It Works

4

People speak generally of bankruptcy without realizing that there are several different types of bankruptcy that operate quite differently. An individual or a corporation can apply for a Chapter 7 or Chapter 11 bankruptcy. Only an individual can apply for a Chapter 13 bankruptcy. In bankruptcy, an individual, but not a corporation, can *exempt* (protect) certain property necessary to live—normally shelter, personal property, and transportation. These, however, are often quite limited protections. See Appendix B for more information on this.

Chapter 7 Bankruptcy

Chapter 7 bankruptcy is the type of bankruptcy most people think about when they speak of bankruptcy. It can be filed by either an individual or a corporation. It will wipe out many debts in their entirety. Thus, if your business owes $40,000 on credit cards, medical bills, and supplier obligations, Chapter 7 bankruptcy would completely eliminate these debts. Some debts—such as certain taxes, secured loans, student loans, and spousal support—are not wiped out. You must continue to make payments on your home if you wish to keep it, and you will generally need to pay money for owed back taxes or make arrangements with the taxing authority.

The trade-off for the clean, relatively debt-free, fresh start that a Chapter 7 bankruptcy provides is that some of your personal and business assets can be taken and sold by the court to partially fulfill some of your debt. The money from the sale of your assets is distributed to your creditors. However, there are exceptions to this rule that in many cases will keep you from losing most of your property.

Each person who files a Chapter 7 bankruptcy will, depending on what state he or she lives in, have a list of the property and dollar limits he or she can keep despite filing for bankruptcy. In most cases, this will mean that the debtor keeps his or her home, furniture, cars, and personal property. Of course, since these items are often *security* (collateral) for debt, the property must still be paid for in monthly payments as was originally contracted, as *secured goods*. On the other hand, business assets are not generally protected, and bankruptcy filers often end up losing their business equipment and supplies. This is true whether or not the business is incorporated.

Chapter 11 Bankruptcy

When one reads in the newspaper about a business filing for bankruptcy, it is usually a *Chapter 11 bankruptcy*. Thus, most small business owners, and indeed many nonbusiness owners, think of Chapter 11 when they think of bankruptcy. These bankruptcies are items you will hear or read about in the news because they affect a great number of people, many jobs are at stake, and many other businesses have business relationships with the entity filing bankruptcy.

An individual, as well as a business, can file a Chapter 11 bankruptcy. However, for reasons we shall discuss, a Chapter 11 bankruptcy is often not suitable for a small business. There are several problems with Chapter 11 bankruptcy from the point of view of a small business owner.

First, the same basic steps must be followed and reported completed regardless of whether you own a huge, national company or a small, single-store operation, which makes Chapter 11 bankruptcy quite expensive.

The second problem is that the underlying purpose of a Chapter 11 bankruptcy is to allow the company time to renegotiate fixed contracts and dispose of unprofitable assets in an orderly way. If you own a single-person operation in which you sell your skills—as a painter or a lawyer, for example—there are unlikely to be fixed contracts to renegotiate or unprofitable assets to give away. If you have only one store location that is not generating sufficient sales to cover your expenses or earn a profit, the problem is your core business, not the contracts or extra locations.

In a Chapter 11 bankruptcy, the business owner files for bankruptcy to stop collection efforts by creditors. The business continues to operate under the direction of the court. Often, the management of the business stays in place and runs the business while the details of the bankruptcy are worked out.

The main trouble with filing a Chapter 11 bankruptcy for a small business is that the rules and procedures are designed for large businesses, like a national airline or manufacturer.

When a Chapter 11 bankruptcy is filed, the lawyers of the creditors often come into court to try to protect the creditors, and you must often pay your own lawyer large sums of money to fight your creditors' lawyers. Since the court has taken control of your business assets, this requires you to file special periodic reports explaining the ongoing financial health of your business and what the managers are doing. This often requires special accountants and always takes a great deal of your manager's time. Normally, a bankruptcy lawyer will require a very large payment up front before he or she undertakes a case to file for Chapter 11 bankruptcy because of the system's complexity, the stringent drafting requirements, and the many trips to court.

The whole process is designed to establish a *plan of reorganization*. The plan of reorganization will detail how each group or *class* of creditors is to be treated and who will receive what. Each class of creditors then votes on the plan. The plan is approved only if it meets a number of complex rules, which are beyond the scope of this short overview. The plan must receive the approval of a certain number of the classes. This is very different from a Chapter 7 bankruptcy, where approval of the creditors is not required.

Of course, no lawyer would draw up a plan and present it for a vote without finding out how key members of the different groups are likely to vote. There is often a great deal of talking among the lawyers for the bankruptcy filer and the different creditors, all of which costs money.

The need for a team of accountants, lawyers, and managers to deal with the bankruptcy issues does not matter all that much to a Fortune 500 company, but it will swamp a small business. For this reason small businesses seldom file a Chapter 11 bankruptcy, and those who do often end up converting to a Chapter 7 bankruptcy.

Chapter 12 Bankruptcy

Congress has enacted the *Chapter 12 bankruptcy* provisions to meet the special problems faced by farmers. A farmer has expenses every month, but the income from the sale of animals, fruits, and grains typically comes only once or twice a year. While the farmer is a small business owner, most small business owners are not farmers. Therefore, a Chapter 12 bankruptcy will not apply to the overwhelming majority of business owners.

Chapter 13 Bankruptcy

Chapter 13 bankruptcy is often called a *wage-earner plan* or a *debt-consolidation plan*. It was originally set up for people who have a steady regular income and who could, if given time, pay at least a portion of their debts. Gradually, the protection of a Chapter 13 bankruptcy was expanded to include people who did not have a steady income—for example, salespeople and waitstaff.

In a Chapter 13 bankruptcy, the debtor discloses his or her income and sets up a plan for paying creditors over a three- to five-year period. The debtor is not as likely to have assets at risk of being taken, like he or she would under a Chapter 7 bankruptcy, because money is being paid to the creditors. The steady monthly payments—often made through an automatic wage deduction—that the debtor makes to the Chapter 13 trustee are distributed to the different creditors in accordance with a plan of repayment that the debtor filed with the bankruptcy court. In these ways, a Chapter 13 bankruptcy is a lot like a Chapter 11 bankruptcy.

Comparing the Types of Bankruptcy

The main difference between a Chapter 11 bankruptcy and a Chapter 13 bankruptcy is one of scale and oversight. Because Chapter 13 bankruptcy deals with smaller dollar amounts and so many of them are filed, there is less oversight by the court and often less involvement by the creditors.

In the regulatory system set up by Congress, there are provisions for continuing to operate large businesses (Chapter 11), farms (Chapter 12), and for individual workers (Chapter 13), but there is nothing designed for the special problem of small business owners. This means that a small business entrepreneur who wants to keep on running a business must try to fit into the provisions of a Chapter 13 bankruptcy or a Chapter 11 bankruptcy, or file a Chapter 7 bankruptcy and start over. Which type of bankruptcy a small business owner files depends on his or her goals. If he or she is willing to give up personal and business assets, he or she would choose a Chapter 7 bankruptcy. If the small business owner wishes to keep running the business, his or her only options are a Chapter 11 or Chapter 13 bankruptcy. As noted before, a Chapter 11 bankruptcy is not a realistic option for most small business owners. This leaves a Chapter 13 bankruptcy—the wage earner's plan.

In a Chapter 13 bankruptcy, the small business owner works out how much profit the business makes after paying business expenses—rent, gas, supplies, etc. This profit is then applied to pay both personal living expenses and money to the court—the *Chapter 13 trustee*—for payment to creditors.

THE INTERPLAY OF BUSINESS AND PERSONAL DEBT

5

Businesses need credit. Supplies have to be ordered and money is needed to tide the business over until customers pay for the goods or services provided, but few creditors will loan money to a small business without a *personal guarantee* from the business owner. Thus the business's and the proprietor's finances rapidly become intertwined. This connection comes at several stages.

When the business is just beginning, tools, equipment, and supplies have to be purchased in order for the business to have a product to sell. The ultimate source of the funds for these expenditures is the money and credit of the proprietor. He or she, in turn, has only a few sources of funds. A few people will have personal savings or relatives and friends who are willing to invest enough to buy these goods outright. Most aspiring small business owners will need to borrow from a bank or other financial institution. As noted earlier, banks will not make a loan without some guarantee. A few people will have sufficient credit standing to obtain *unsecured loans* (getting money without collateral), but most will need to pledge an asset such as the business equipment, their home, car, etc. Landlords will typically require that individuals sign leases, rather than having the lease only in a company name.

Then, there is the *start-up phase*. Most businesses do the work and get paid when the work is completely or partially finished. Unless the business is a part-time or second job type of operation, this means taking on more debt to tide you over until the funds start coming in. This phase can last a long time. It is not uncommon for a business to be unprofitable for as much as a year or two. During this period, proprietors often turn to credit cards, or if they are lucky, draw on a line of credit secured by their start-up loan.

The next period when personal and business finances become intertwined is while the business is operating successfully. Proprietors will often begin using a company car for their transportation. They may buy items like cars, tools, trucks, and computers themselves and take them to the business operation for use by the business. Many times it is very hard to reconstruct what belongs to whom. The proprietor will forget he or she bought the car he or she is driving in the company name, or that the company work truck was bought by him or her personally.

At least with vehicles there are titles to look at. With computers, office equipment, and work tools, it is much harder. For example, proprietors often go to the computer store and pay for the computer personally and take it to the office, or they may take a computer bought with company funds home for personal use.

The next stage is when the business begins to hit rough spots. It is the end of the week or the month and there is not enough money for payroll. The proprietor may have only one source of money—his or her personal bank account. Even if the business has enough money for the payroll, the proprietor's family must be fed and his or her personal bills paid. If the business is not generating enough to cover this, the proprietor will have to use personal funds to tide him or her over. If he or she is lucky, he or she can do so by drawing money out of savings. If not, he or she must use a credit card or a line of credit. Typically, the proprietor has difficulty obtaining a loan to cover expenses during these business slowdowns, either because a bank will not loan to someone who does not have good cash flow or because it will take too long for a loan to go through.

The last stage is when slow times become chronic. There is too little money coming in for too many periods of time. Of course expenses are cut, but one can cut only so deep without killing the business. Somewhere along the way, proprietors often make a mistake that will be discussed further in Section 9, especially if it has been a long time since the proprietor paid him- or herself or took a draw and personal credit is exhausted. All too often, the proprietor does not forward sales tax to the government or does not send the money withheld from employee payrolls. This creates a personal liability for the proprietor and officers of the company, and it creates another debt—this time to the government. Or sometimes owners will not file their income taxes, figuring they can cross the bridge of tax liability when they get the business back on its feet.

In addition to business-connected debts, the proprietor also has the same situations that create debt as the rest of the general public. Proprietors have marriages break up, or they or their family members get sick and accrue doctor and hospital bills. Their cars break down, furnaces give out, and roofs leak. All of these circumstances put a strain on the owner's personal finances. And it is the owner's personal financial health that is often the underpinning for the business cash reserve. If something like this happens in the proprietor's personal life, the business may be starved for money or attention. An owner who is home sick or injured cannot run a business.

For these reasons, a small business owner is much more likely to have money problems than a person working for a wage or salary.

FOURTEEN MYTHS ABOUT DEBT AND BANKRUPTCY

6

When people consider bankruptcy for themselves or their business, they experience all sorts of vague fears based on snippets of information they have heard over the years, advice from well-meaning friends and family members, and the rising of their own fears and concerns.

The most common concerns are:

- it will ruin my credit;

- notice of my bankruptcy will be put in the newspaper and become public;

- it will ruin my spouse's credit;

- I will lose my home and cars;

- I will lose all of my other property;

- they will sell my property at auction in front of my home;

- if I file bankruptcy, my spouse will have to file also;

- my spouse and I will lose our jobs;

- I will lose my license;

- I will not be able to get student loans;

- I will not be able to have a bank account;

- I will be put in jail if I do not pay my bills;

- the debts will go away in time; and,

- I will never have credit again.

It Will Ruin My Credit

It is not uncommon for people considering bankruptcy to have very good credit. Over the years, they have been careful to pay their bills on time, and as a consequence have been able to borrow large sums of money. Then something happens—a loss of income, an illness, an injury, or a divorce. Because of one or more of these, they begin to have trouble paying their bills on time. Often people will hold off financial problems by dipping into their savings and selling assets. But the day still comes when they do not have the funds to make their monthly payments for debts.

Normally people hold on, hoping for a turn of tides as the collection calls from creditors increase in volume and harshness. In most cases it is only then that people begin to think about bankruptcy and seek out the advice of a lawyer.

Reading about bankruptcy or seeing a lawyer is a symptom of financial problems. If a person concludes bankruptcy is the only way to address his or her financial problems, it is not the bankruptcy that is going to ruin his or her credit. The person's credit status is already in trouble. To put it in medical terms, a fever is not what makes you sick—the fever is a symptom of an underlying bodily illness or injury. Bankruptcy is the financial fever and is the symptom of the underlying financial problem. A bankruptcy notation on your credit report is a strong negative, but so are car repossessions, home foreclosures, many late payments, and a high debt load. The key is to see if you are any worse off with a bankruptcy.

Notice of My Bankruptcy Will Be Put in the Newspaper and Become Public

People are embarrassed when they face financial problems. Having financial problems is often viewed as a prime capitalist sin. They want their financial affairs to be strictly private. For this reason, they often worry that the fact they filed for bankruptcy will be put in the newspaper.

Rest assured that there is almost no chance your personal bankruptcy will end up in the newspaper. When the newspaper features stories on bankruptcies, the stories are almost always about large companies with many employees and suppliers—the type of thing that will interest a broad readership. Your personal bankruptcy filing is of limited interest to readers and not worth the limited space a newspaper has in its daily or weekly edition. In theory, the bankruptcy of a well-known small business could cause a press story. In reality, though, this almost never happens.

However, one cannot entirely rule out the possibility that the news would be put in the paper. Some small local papers are very hard up for items to put in the paper and could choose to print the filing of your bankruptcy. Bankruptcy filings are public records and someone can go to the bankruptcy courthouse and look up bankruptcy filings. However, even then the odds are very low. Bankruptcy courts cover a very large population base and normally many counties are under the jurisdiction of the court. This means a very large number of filings would have to be searched to locate the ones that would have any possible significance to the few readers of the small local paper, which is not a good use of the newspaper's limited resources.

Another factor protecting your privacy is that most newspapers view this type of personal problem as beyond the scope of what a newspaper should cover. Newspapers are not gossip sheets or purveyors of personal problems.

A business owner faces only slightly more risk of having his or her personal financial affairs made public. If it turns out you file for personal bankruptcy, the previous discussion will likely apply to you also. Of course, when your business is no longer open or supplying services, customers will know something is wrong. But, they are unlikely to know exactly what is wrong. Businesses close all the time—sometimes because finances overwhelmed them and sometimes because it is no longer worth the owner's effort to keep the business going because the business is just not making sufficient money to satisfy the owner. The customer will never know which it is and thus will never know the full story.

In some bankruptcy cases, the business has assets that the trustee will try to sell either at a liquidation sale or by auction. However, it takes a fairly large business with a high number of assets to make either one of those procedures worthwhile to the trustee. It takes time and money to hold a sale or an auction of goods. Most small businesses do not have enough property to make a special sale of the business, inventory, or assets cost effective for the trustee. He or she is much more likely to sell the items by private sale through a private network. He or she will sell to buyers he or she has developed relationships with or sell the items as part of a larger auction of many items from many different sources.

We must reiterate, however, that bankruptcies are *matters of public record.* This means there will be a file at the bankruptcy courthouse that can be examined by any member of the public. The same is true of the records of most lawsuits at the county courthouse. But accessing these records is not easy. There are too many for someone to just thumb through, and they must have your specific name to pull your file. This makes it very unlikely that a friend or neighbor will just stumble upon your file. And of course, there is the time and effort involved in physically going to the courthouse—something almost no one is willing to take the trouble to do.

There is a movement underway to allow access to court and bankruptcy records through the Internet. This removes one barrier of finding out about bankruptcy—the physical effort. The records can be reached from a home or business. However, doing this search online is not very easy either. The layout of the web page is government-designed and is not made for ease of use. It takes a great deal more effort to navigate the website than most people are willing to undertake. It is not designed for browsing. You must have a specific name or case number to pull up a file. This makes it unlikely that anyone will, by accident, stumble upon the fact that you filed for bankruptcy.

Some businesses systematically go through bankruptcy filings for their own commercial purposes. Credit unions do this. Some banks or groups of banks collect this information. Credit card companies, lenders, and mortgage brokers also systematically search the bankruptcy records. Their purpose is to make offers to you for credit cards or new loans. Thus, to summarize, as far as publishing the filing of your bankruptcy, the most likely result will be that you find yourself on additional mailing lists for credit cards and loans.

It Will Ruin My Spouse's Credit

People are naturally worried about their spouse or future spouses. They say things like, "My wife (or husband) had nothing to do with the business—I don't want their credit hurt," or, "I'm about to get married. Will the bankruptcy affect my spouse's credit?" (A variation of the last question is, "Will my spouse be responsible for my debts?")

Barring a mistake on the part of the credit bureau or a creditor, spouses are not affected if one member of a marriage files or has filed bankruptcy. Each person has a separate file at the credit bureau and is tracked by his or her Social Security number. Thus, assuming the spouse is not a codebtor, a person's bankruptcy should not affect the credit of his or her spouse.

Some creditors will try to tell a spouse that he or she must pay this debt because he or she is married to the debtor. This is only a collection tactic that takes advantage of people's lack of knowledge about the law.

Occasionally a debt or bankruptcy will show up reported on a spouse's credit file. This is almost always removed when the spouse objects to the entry because there is no legal basis for such a claim. Furthermore, the creditor and credit bureau can get sued if this error is not corrected.

Of course, if the spouse (or other family member) is a codebtor, then the debt and the bankruptcy will affect the spouse (or other family member). Each codebtor is responsible for all the debt, and if one does not pay, the creditors can take collection efforts against the other codebtor.

I Will Lose My Home and Cars

This is a realistic possibility depending on what state you live in. Most states allow people who file bankruptcy to retain a home and a car up to a specific value. For example, in Texas and Florida the allowed value of a home is unlimited, while in Delaware and Pennsylvania there are no home exemptions allowed. Most states' exemptions range from $5,000 to $30,000. This is free equity in the home, so the amount of any mortgage must be deducted from the market value to obtain the free value of the house. Clearly, if you own your home free of all debt you will (in most states) lose it in bankruptcy. But most business owners, between starting their business and trying to keep it afloat, borrow against their homes before considering bankruptcy, so their free equity in the home is limited.

The protection is offered to people's main residence, so you cannot claim an exemption on vacation homes and rental property.

Cars work the same way. Most states allow you to keep one vehicle. Most states allow between $1,000 and $5,000 in free value for your vehicle. It is not uncommon to see business owners at the end of their financial rope who still own cars and trucks free and clear. These people will be faced with the prospect of giving up their vehicles or borrowing money from family members to pay the trustee the difference between the exemption amount and the value of the vehicle.

The protection is normally offered to one vehicle per person, so if you own several cars (including cars used by your children), you stand to lose those extra cars, unless there are loans against them for more than their value.

I Will Lose All of My Other Property

This is a constant fear people have. Much of what a bankruptcy lawyer does is define what property could possibly be taken by the bankruptcy court system and what could not. Most small business owners who file *personal bankruptcy* will not lose any of their personal property, as every state allows a bankruptcy filer to keep *personal property* (furniture, clothes, appliances, etc.) with which to get a fresh start. The great majority of our filers lose nothing.

However, there are exceptions. These normally come when the person who is filing has more property than the average person—an expensive house filled with fine furniture, business assets, several vehicles that are paid for, vacation or rental houses, collections that have a ready market, antiques, silver collections, expensive paintings, etc. What states allow people to keep is fairly bare-boned; extras and expensive extras are likely to be taken by the bankruptcy system.

They Will Sell My Property at an Auction in Front of My Home

The idea of not only losing one's property but also having it sold in a public way in front of one's neighbors is horrifying. This almost never happens. This misconception seems to come from seeing auctions of farm equipment as part of the television news. Accounts of farmers' bankruptcies and the sale of their equipment are sometimes put on the air as news stories. These sales often happen at the farm. A farm is a business and the farm equipment and livestock have a high value and are hard to physically move. It makes economic sense to hold a sale where these items are physically located. The same is true of a store's inventory—although these sales often owe more to marketing hype than the bankruptcy process.

We have never seen a case where the trustee had household goods of such value that he or she would dream of having a sale at a person's house. It is far more effective to hold any sale of personal property at a central sales location where buyers are used to coming to purchase items. And of course, since the great majority of personal property is never taken and sold, there would be no sale in the first place.

It is possible, but unlikely, to have a home sold at public auction. This happens when a person files for bankruptcy, gives up his or her home, and the mortgages against it are so low that there will be something for the trustee to recover if he or she has an auction of the home. In such a case, the trustee is likely to put ads in the newspaper saying a house at a given address will be sold at auction as part of the bankruptcy of "Joe Doe." The reason this does not happen in most cases is that people are careful to not file bankruptcy if they will run the risk of having their home taken from them by the trustee.

If I File Bankruptcy, My Spouse Will Have to File Also

Small business owners often fear bankruptcy because they worry about dragging their spouse into bankruptcy. They think that if one member of the marriage files, the other must also file. This is not correct. Bankruptcy is an individual process, and one spouse files without the other all the time. However, spouses often find it makes sense to file together as both owe money to the same creditors. To have just one file in such a case would merely throw the debts back on the other.

In many cases, both spouses are not liable for the debts. One spouse may have operated the business and only the other spouse actually signed the loans. Or one of the spouses may have incurred the debts before the marriage, so the debt is only in that person's name. In such cases, one individual filing makes sense and is desirable. Having only one spouse file leaves the other spouse without debt and without a bankruptcy on his or her credit history.

But remember, while the debt is often in only one spouse's name, many of the assets are in both names. Make a careful examination of property owned and its value before a spouse files bankruptcy alone, just as you would if you filed jointly. Also, understand that the nonfiling spouse's income must be counted—subject to his or her own offsets—in working out the filing spouse's *means test.*

My Spouse and I Will Lose Our Jobs

This is a real concern for people. Many small business owners run their business as a sideline to a day job—or have spouses who work. People do not automatically lose their jobs if they file bankruptcy and the employer learns of it. In fact, it is illegal to terminate someone because he or she filed for bankruptcy. Most employers never know that you filed for bankruptcy. Those who do know will often be glad you have addressed the financial problems that were disturbing you and causing you to receive collection phone calls at work. In addition, the employer may feel safer. Sometimes people embezzle money from employers in an effort to pay their debts. This temptation is gone if the debts have been addressed through declaring bankruptcy.

It must be said, however, that there are some employers who do not look with favor on a bankruptcy filing. Normally these are employers in the financial industry. They are the ones who lose money because of bankruptcy and naturally do not look with favor on the process. Others are in the business of handling customers' money and feel it does not look good if their employees let their personal finances get away from them.

I Will Lose My License

The government regulates many activities. It issues driver's licenses and licenses to engage in certain professions—for example, for barbers, insurance salespeople, doctors, contractors, and stockbrokers.

Some businesses involve licenses to handle other people's money—such as for insurance salespeople, financial managers, and stockbrokers. The majority of these people have not lost their licenses because of filing bankruptcy, and many have obtained licenses in some of these fields after bankruptcy. However, a blanket statement cannot be made, as these licenses are normally issued by the individual states and local governments. The rules can vary greatly from one area to another, and many of these rules may require disclosure of a bankruptcy filing. Just to be safe, it is a good idea to ask about the licensing agency's policies before you file for bankruptcy.

I Will Not Be Able to Get Student Loans

College and graduate school are very important. People often worry that they or their children will not be able to obtain student loans if they file bankruptcy. This fear is overblown. Loans for college and graduate school come from two sources. One is government-guaranteed student loan pools and the other is private borrowing that is to be used to pay for schooling. Government-guaranteed student loans—the great majority of loans used for schooling—are not affected by a bankruptcy.

Borrowing from banks based solely on your credit is another matter. These loans, like any other loan, will be affected for several years until you rebuild your credit.

I Will Not Be Able to Have a Bank Account

A person who is in bankruptcy or who has filed bankruptcy in the past is not prevented by law from having a checking or savings account with a bank or financial institution. Not being able to have a bank account is a common fear among people considering bankruptcy, and it is hard to see where the myth got started. Perhaps it arises from a garbled version of some real considerations concerning bank accounts in bankruptcy.

If you have a bank account with a bank you owe money to, it is often advisable to close that bank account or keep an amount of no more than a few dollars in it. This is because the banks that have money owed to them can freeze accounts and collect the money to pay off the debt owed to them. This is called the *right of offset*. This means that if a person holds money for you, and you owe that person money because of a debt, that person can dip into the money he or she is holding for you to satisfy that debt. For this reason people going through bankruptcy often close their bank accounts at the bank or credit union they have been doing business with.

The other possible source of the myth is that some people find it hard to open a new bank account after they have filed bankruptcy. Banks do not have to do business with you and some choose not to deal with people who have filed bankruptcy. However, banking is a competitive business and people can usually find a bank to deal with after their filing—they just have to work a little harder and perhaps go to a bank location that is less convenient for them.

I Will Be Put in Jail if I Do Not Pay My Bills

Fear of jail or arrest because a bill is not paid is not unusual among people who cannot pay their debts. Bill collectors often play on this fear by threatening that they will send the sheriff out to see the debtor if the bill is not paid. Rest assured that no one is ever put in jail for simply owing money. This might have happened hundreds of years ago, but not in the modern United States. Debt is what is called a *civil matter*—it is between two people or businesses and does not involve the government. It is not a breach of government rules (such as murder or robbery), so the government cannot send you to jail for it.

The Debts Will Go Away in Time

If you cannot be jailed for debt, why file bankruptcy at all? After all, debts show up on your credit report for only seven years and you do not own anything of value—why even consider bankruptcy?

If you own little property, you are what lawyers call *judgment proof*. That is, a judgment can be taken against you, but there is nothing to collect against. Some states allow wage garnishment to collect on a private civil debt, but some do not.

This being the case, particularly if you live in a nongarnishment state or have irregular income, why worry about the debts? There are a few reasons.

- Just because the debt is removed from your credit report does not mean that you no longer owe the debt. The obligation to pay a debt can easily last longer than seven years.

- The creditor can obtain a judgment against you. This has several effects. It will extend the time the obligation shows up on your credit report and will extend the life of the obligation.

- The judgment becomes a *judgment lien.* If you should acquire a home or land in the locale where the judgment is docketed, the judgment will attach itself to it. When you go to transfer the property, the buyer will normally require that the judgment plus interest be paid. In this way the debt and judgment limit your ability to get back on your feet and move ahead. Judgment liens do not go away for a long time, and in fact, as your land or home becomes more valuable, judgment liens may allow the creditor to seize the property.

A creditor obtaining a judgment starts the seven-year credit report clock running again. The applicable time period on your credit report is not just seven years from the original debt, but seven years from the last major debt activity.

I Will Never Have Credit Again

Simply put, this is not true. It may take some time and effort on your part, but you can have access to credit again. Section 19 covers this subject in detail.

ALTERNATIVES TO BANKRUPTING YOUR BUSINESS OR YOURSELF

Most people go through four different stages as they face financial hard times and before they consider filing for bankruptcy.

1. They try to lower their expenses or borrow additional funds to tide themselves over.

2. They attempt to deal with collection efforts by explaining their situation to the creditors and collectors, and they try to work with the creditors to arrange lower payments.

3. They consider a credit service that will attempt to work with their creditors for them.

4. They talk with a bankruptcy lawyer.

This is a logical sequence of responses, but people often tend to rush through some stages and spend too much time in others.

Working with business creditors is much the same as working with personal creditors, but there is one key difference—you are also a customer as well as a debtor to your suppliers as a business owner. For this reason you are likely to be dealt with more gently than by a consumer debt collection agent who is collecting on an account his or her company bought.

Budget

Stage one is a particular problem for small business owners. They often are faced with trying to trim business expenses and personal expenses at the same time. This is often done without drawing up detailed budgets for either their business or personal accounts.

This is a huge mistake. The importance of budgets cannot be overstated. The income of many small businesses will vary from month to month but this should not preclude making a budget for expenses. Expenses also vary from month to month, with taxes, insurance, and heating costs being higher in some months than in others. But by going over several months' or years' bills, you can develop a monthly average. This will form the basis for your future decisions and calculations. Appendix A has some typical household and business categories that you can use as a template for developing your budget.

With a budget outlined you can make decisions on where to cut spending. On the personal side, you will find that there are only a few places you can cut. Food, clothing, and entertainment are typically the first to be cut. Items like house and car payments, on the other hand, are fixed expenses and are missed only at the risk of causing severe problems.

If you are to the point where you are skipping house or car payments or are not paying taxes, you have severe problems and are likely beyond making simple expense adjustments.

Similar considerations hold true on the business side. Some expenses will be fixed—Yellow Page ads, phone bills, rent, and tool payments. Others can be varied—newspaper ads, bonuses, or your salary.

Borrowing and Debt Consolidation

Your House

We often see many people, both business owners and individual employees, who have lost their homes or are four to eight months behind on their house payments. When asked how they got so far behind, many tell the same story: they were working on getting a loan on their house to refinance it and the loan never came through, or when it came through it was much more expensive than they had been told. Often people are presented with these higher interest rates and high closing fee loans when they go to closing. At that time they have no choice but to take the loan; they are months behind on their original loan and the creditors want all of their money in one lump payment right away. The people must either take the new high-cost loan or lose their house.

These people have been the victims of unscrupulous loan brokers. There is a great deal of money to be made by matching up a lender and a borrower. Of course, this money can only be made if a borrower will wait around while the broker tries different lenders. Sometimes a match is made right away; sometimes it takes a long time. If it does take a long time, it is very important to the broker to keep the borrower available. Some unscrupulous brokers get business by promising everyone who calls them that there is a very good chance they will get the loan. This gets the borrower tied in with them. Then they tell all types of stories about missing papers, people out sick, etc., to keep the borrower from trying something else.

Before you borrow against your home, keep these three simple facts in mind.

1. Do not borrow against your house to pay credit card or other unsecured debts. Most people do not solve their debt problems by doing this. After all, their house payments go up and they are exchanging debt that a lawyer or consumer credit counselor can do something about for

a house mortgage that no one can do anything about. You must pay every cent on time or you will lose your house.

2. It normally takes about a week or two after you provide your information to know whether or not you obtained the loan. Never wait more than thirty days to find out about a loan. If you wait longer than that, see a lawyer or consumer credit counselor at once.

3. Do not pay any attention to how nice brokers are. They are always nice. The real test is: did they get you the loan in a reasonable period of time? If not, see a lawyer or consumer credit counselor about your money problems.

WARNING

If your house is being foreclosed on, see an attorney at once. You do not have time to get—and probably cannot afford—a refinanced loan. Do not pay any attention to a loan broker who tells you not to worry about the foreclosure. The loan broker may not be able to take care of the problem. Too many people have lost their homes while waiting for someone who told him or her not to worry. It does not matter to a broker if you lose your house, but he or she may make money off of you if you stick around during delays in your processing.

Disadvantages to borrowing against your home. It is a high-risk gamble to borrow against your home to pay off other debts. It sounds so logical. Replace your many high interest rate credit card payments with one low tax deductible payment.

Keep in mind what you are doing.

- You are making a bet. If you lose the bet, you lose your home. The bet is that you will not have any more credit card debt after you refinance your house. Many of the people who refinance to pay off credit cards go back and run up new charges on their cards. Now they have two debts, a big house payment, and credit card payments on top of that.

- You are betting that nothing bad will happen to you. You assume you will not have a drop in income, you or your family members will not get sick and miss work, and you will not have big medical bills. You assume you and your mate will not split up or that you will not have to take on the care of a parent, child, or grandchild. If one of these things happens and you are maxed out on your home debt because of refinancing, then you are in danger of losing your home.

- You have exchanged a debt that would be paid off in the short term by making maximum payments for one you are likely to be paying for twenty-five or thirty years.

- You have exchanged a debt that a bankruptcy lawyer or consumer credit counselor can do something about for one that cannot be modified.

Your Retirement Fund

Another thing many people do when they have financial problems is borrow against their retirement money. This is a terrible idea.

Something can be done about most debts—even houses that are being foreclosed on—but once your retirement money is gone, it is gone. Social Security will not be enough to retire on. If you spend your retirement money, you will not be able to retire and you will have to work when you are older. There are not many jobs for older people. This is why one sees so many senior citizens supplementing their incomes by working at jobs that teenagers used to do, such as bagging groceries and working at fast food restaurants. You may think your children will help you, but your kids may have financial problems of their own.

Hold on to your retirement money. Before you even think about taking money out of your retirement account because of money problems, see a bankruptcy lawyer or consumer credit counselor.

Consolidation

Many people feel that if they could just get a *debt consolidation loan*, they could come through their financial crisis. The idea of exchanging many payments for one is seductive. Unfortunately, this is seldom the answer to people's financial problems.

Financial institutions are often reluctant to loan money to people who are having financial problems because of a drop in income. They will look at a potential borrower's cash flow to see if the monthly loan payments can be made. Far too often there is little or no income to make the loan payments.

They will also look at the potential borrower's *debt-to-income ratio* (a number computed by dividing your income by your debt). If you already have high debts, a lender is unlikely to give you money so you can pay off other lenders.

Even if you can obtain a debt consolidation loan while you are experiencing a financial crisis, you are likely to be charged a high interest rate. This will make paying off a new loan harder and it will take longer. In addition, the higher interest rate will mean your total monthly payments on the one loan are unlikely to be smaller than the sum of your other loans.

Dealing with Creditors

As noted in Section 3, dealing with creditors can be one of the worst experiences of your life. They are all too often rude, threatening, and abusive. On the personal side, people often attempt to explain why they are not able to pay their bills and try to make arrangements to make partial payments. They often go so far as to call all their creditors and carefully and logically explain their situation and try to make partial payments for a while. This is usually a waste of time and emotional energy.

The collection process typically relies on teams of collectors working accounts. You may have a long conversation with one collector and work something out, and two days later a different collector will call and deny any knowledge of this arrangement, insult you, and demand payment in full.

Even if you are dealing with one creditor, your sincere efforts to explain yourself are not likely to work. Even the most kind-hearted collection agents become hardened after a while. They are lied to quite often and hear false promises from many debtors. In addition, the collection process demands results of the collection workers, and the system seems to have concluded that being rude and unreasonable is more cost-effective than being understanding and taking reduced payments. Thus you may be able, through great effort, to work something out with a few creditors, but the odds of getting all of your creditors to work with you are low.

Trade Creditors

Discussions with *trade creditors* are likely to be more fruitful. Most trade creditors will continue to sell to you on a C.O.D. basis, even if you run into payment problems with them. Selling to businesses is a competitive business and most sellers know that you have other vendors you can go to if they become too harsh.

Workout Program

The next step business owners typically try is a *workout program* brokered by a third party. There are very few groups that do this type of activity for the business debts of very small businesses. There is really not much need since trade creditors tend to deal with you in a logical and businesslike manner.

On the other hand, there is a great need for such third parties when it comes to dealing with personal debt, as collectors on consumer accounts are very aggressive and hard to work with.

There are basically two types of intermediaries to use: Consumer Credit Counseling (CCC) and the nonprofit companies that one often sees and hears advertised on television or the radio.

Consumer Credit Counseling

CCC is a nonprofit organization, often affiliated with the United Way, that is supported in part by the credit industry. Typically you go into its local office and meet face-to-face with a counselor. The charge to you is very low, and much of the financial support for CCC comes from the credit industry and the United Way. The value is high because the counselor, at your individual session, will go over your budget and analyze your debt status.

One great value of CCC is that it will help you look at your personal budget and see what can be changed. CCC will normally set you up on a repayment plan that lasts about three to five years, and you will pay back all the debt plus interest. Often a notation that you were in a CCC program will go on your credit report, but this is probably less damaging to your credit than many late payments, foreclosures, repossessions, or declaring bankruptcy.

For a partial list of local CCC offices and contact information, look at Appendix C.

Other Workout Programs

There are a growing number of other third-party intermediaries. They often go by the names of debt counselors or debt consolidation agencies. Their infomercials and ads are common on television and radio. They are typically labeled in their advertisements as nonprofit companies. However, one must understand what is meant by *nonprofit*. The term *nonprofit* does not mean they do not make money. They often make very good money and their employees can earn a high salary. The term *nonprofit* means that no profits are paid out (it is all spent on operating costs and salaries), or there are no shareholders who are entitled to profits. These companies typically make their money by charging you a handling fee. Or, they obtain an agreement with the creditor to let them have part of the money collected in exchange for collecting monthly payments from you and sending them to the creditors.

They say they will work out a deal with your creditors where you make one payment to them as debt adjustor and they will in turn pay your creditors. Unlike lawyers or the Credit Bureau, many of these operators are not licensed or regulated, so there are no limits on what they can do.

A few merely take your money and do not send it to anyone, so after months of faithfully making your payments you are out your money and still have the debts. Many are able to make arrangements with some, but not all, of your creditors. This means some creditors will still be calling you. Others may take your money and make minimum payments to your creditors—after taking a cut for themselves. At the rate they make payments for you, it could be many years before your debts are paid off.

WARNING

Be very careful of anyone who does not have a local office you can go to. Go to that office before you send them any of your money. Find out if it is regulated by your state or a United Way agency. If not, be careful dealing with that company.

If you use such a service, you should track what is happening to your loans very carefully. All too often, people think things are going fine. They are making their monthly payments and the phone calls from creditors have largely stopped. It is only after several months that they learn their loan balances have not gone down. Ask specifically how long the payments will take to pay off your debt, because they are charging you each month and the organization may have an incentive to keep you in the plan as long as possible.

Lawyers, Business Creditors, and Their Functions | 8

Lawyers are often given a bad reputation. Many times, to an outsider, it seems that what the lawyers are doing are routine actions that could be done by anyone with a little common sense. At other times, it seems that the lawyers are making the whole process unduly complicated. Like many stereotypes, there are some elements of truth in these claims—and much that is not true.

There is an old story about a factory owner whose key machine broke down and the whole plant could not run. The company repairperson could not fix the problem, and at last, in desperation, the owner called in an outside mechanic. The mechanic said it would cost five hundred dollars to do a diagnostic and fix the machine, and the owner desperately agreed. The mechanic looked at the machine a few minutes and then opened the machine and replaced a belt and toggle switch. He then presented his bill. The owner was indignant, saying, "Five hundred dollars for those simple steps is outrageous. I could have done that." The mechanic said, "You are not paying for the replacement work, but for my knowing which belt and switch to replace. Besides, your factory is up and running again with a minimum of loss, so you have saved thousands of dollars."

That is what you are paying for when you hire a lawyer to work on your business financial issues. You are not paying him or her just to fill out forms, but also for the knowledge of what will and will not work in a complicated system.

The bankruptcy system is complicated partly because the laws often use compromising language that no one fully realized would produce the results it did. This wording is then thought about by smart people who examine every word and its relationship to the other words.

The lawyers who do bankruptcy cases every day live in the world of this bankruptcy speak—they know what *reasonable* means in their courts and just how *fair market value* is calculated. Much of the paperwork is routine. But often, business cases are not simple, and this is why lawyers have a larger place in business bankruptcies. You, the client and consumer, also have a place, and you can benefit greatly by understanding in a general way what is going on. The lawyer may know the law and the local court customs, but you know your personal situation far better than the lawyer ever will. The lawyer uses questions and forms to try to collect all the pertinent facts, but these systems have flaws. He or she knows exactly what he or she means when asking you how many mortgages you have against your home. But you must know that a line of credit secured by your house is considered a mortgage to answer this question correctly.

It is suggested that when you start to have cash flow problems you see a lawyer fairly early in the process. If you have read this book carefully, you will know some of the major traps to avoid as you work to save your business and your personal finances. There may be other traps that are specific to your situation that a lawyer can help you with.

Workouts

A major step in saving any business is a *workout*. You and the lawyer, if you use one, are likely to be more successful if the creditor knows you understand your rights in these negotiations. The end game is bankruptcy. The creditor will (or should know that it will) receive little or nothing if you have to file bankruptcy. Because of this, it is sometimes possible for the creditor to become something like a partner as you both work to find a way to avoid the catastrophe to each of you involved in you filing bankruptcy.

First you must know who is worth dealing with. Consumer debt—medical bills, credit cards, etc.—are not good candidates for workouts. From the creditor's point of view, the amounts involved are fairly small. The credit industry seems to have made a calculation that it is more cost effective to have some debtors go bankrupt than to undergo the expense of hiring people to spend time trying to resolve the debt crisis.

Business debts are very different. To a business owner creditor, the debt of a small business operation like yours may be a major one. And if he or she can keep you alive on a reasonable basis, you represent future sales to him or her.

At first he or she may not appreciate the gravity of the situation and will often treat your protestations of money problems with a grain of salt. Creditors hear this type of thing all the time. They are likely to tell you that you must pay in full at once with no excuses.

However, the dynamics often change when a lawyer is brought in and starts explaining the ramifications of the problems. Spending money to have a lawyer shows that you are serious and that you have a serious problem—a problem that could result in business death for your company and losses for your creditor—might mean that you are taken more seriously.

What will often follow is a dance where your lawyer tries to secure breathing room and a continued flow of supplies for you. The business creditor, on the other hand, will try to secure a more protected position should your business fail and have to file bankruptcy.

COD

A common early step is to place your business on *cash on delivery* (COD). You receive your products and the seller is sure to receive money for goods paid for right when he or she delivers them. This puts you in a tight position, but a surprising number of small businesses can live with this procedure. Furthermore, it at least allows them to continue to operate while they address their outstanding debts. This COD solution is such a reflexive step by the creditor that it is often an early warning sign that your financial problems are getting out of hand.

Many times a business cannot survive if it is placed on COD. Its *lead time* between goods received and service on products sold is too long. The business needs continued credit to continue to operate.

Liens

Sellers who know you are in trouble—and who may even have collectibles from you that are not being paid—are understandably reluctant to give you more credit. Your only hope is to offer the seller an improved position in the event you file bankruptcy. What you can offer will depend on your business and what you have already given other creditors. A possible item is a *lien* on your accounts receivable, business equipment, or inventory. This type of action is a fine line for most small businesses to walk. Often they will not have inventory to offer, and equipment may already have a lien on it. Often the creditor does not want to risk taking an interest in your collectibles or equipment because it is not really set up to dispose of them.

Advantages and Possibilities of the Workout

Another possible advantage of a workout guided by a lawyer or other third party is to simply get your creditors off your back. Receiving demanding phone calls from creditors saps your time and energy. Dealing with them takes time away from what you could spend on saving the business. Quite often a phone conversation with a third party who can unemotionally explain the consequences of your business failing to everyone will cause business creditors to back off. They must get something, but if a reasonable case can be made that a little time will allow the business to survive, they may stop the calls and lawsuits.

For a workout to be accepted, you must have a brighter future. A job in the process of being done, a customer almost landed, and an improved economic prospect are all examples of what to present. Entrepreneurs by nature are optimistic. The first person you should try to convince is the lawyer you visit. He or she will tell you whether or not your plan or prospects make sense. Since the business is not your attorney's business, he or she can be more objective about its prospects. While lawyers try to be objective, they do not know as much about your business and your industry as you do, so you may be tempted to bluff on the truth with them. You are paying your lawyer good money for his or her advice and time, so try to be as honest and objective as you can in telling him or her the facts of your situation.

Sometimes the mere mention of bankruptcy will be enough to make the creditors back off a bit and offer compromises. Sometimes it is the mention of bankruptcy by a lawyer that will do it. Other times nothing will stop the creditors and a workout is impossible. You cannot know until you start the process. If a workout is impossible then you will need to consider what will happen if you file bankruptcy.

Ten Traps and Mistakes to Avoid When You Have Money Problems

The small business owner should be thinking about what he or she will do if a business downturn continues too long. In financial affairs, the ultimate retreat is bankruptcy. You want to fight as hard as you can to keep your business and personal finances going, but do so in a way that will leave you an exit strategy if that ultimately becomes necessary.

There are a number of classic mistakes people make when they are facing financial problems—mistakes that make it very hard to salvage their assets when they must consider bankruptcy. Some of the mistakes to avoid are:

- borrowing against a pension plan;

- borrowing against a home to pay off credit cards;

- borrowing from family members and giving a vehicle or home as security;

- taking cash advances on a credit card;

- living off of credit cards;

- transferring balances from one card to another;

- lying or exaggerating on loan applications;

- not paying income taxes;

- stopping payment of withholding; or,

- not following corporate formalities.

Pension Plan Borrowing

One of the worst mistakes a person can make is to borrow against his or her IRA, 401(k), or other retirement account. It is so tempting. You need money and there is a ready source of funds, often quite large, sitting there just waiting for you to draw on it. The program even has a hardship withdrawal provision.

The problem with this course of action is how these withdrawals are treated for tax purposes and in bankruptcy. Retirement investments and savings are given tax-favored treatment because the government wants to encourage savings for people's old age. Further, there are tax penalties for taking the money out too soon. This is why you receive so little of the money if you cash out your retirement account early. Taxes eat up a huge portion of the money you draw out. To avoid this tax you must set up a repayment program.

However, under bankruptcy, retirement loan repayments are often treated as payments to yourself and are not considered as a living expense when computing what you can afford to pay toward your debts. This presents a *Hobson's choice* to the person who has borrowed against his or her retirement savings. When the court calculates income to determine what type of bankruptcy the person must file (Chapter 7 or Chapter 13), if the available money is higher because of this withdrawal, the court can take this into account when determining how much money you can use to repay your debts. However, if bankruptcy takes this money, the retirement loan cannot be paid back. A huge tax liability is triggered by a premature withdrawal from the retirement account. It is an impossible problem. It is better to leave the money in your retirement account and never borrow against it than face this problem.

Borrowing Against a Home to Pay Off Credit Cards

A close second to borrowing against your retirement account is borrowing against your home to pay off credit cards. The ads are so seductive: "Pay off your high interest credit cards with a lower interest second (or third or fourth) loan against your home. The interest payments may even be tax deductible." This sounds like such a good deal that more and more people are taking this very step. This can be a big mistake. Primarily, you are trading debts you can discharge in bankruptcy for a debt you must pay to avoid losing your home.

However, sometimes it can be a good idea. Almost everyone who is considering bankruptcy says, "I don't care what else I lose; I want to save my home." A house is more than shelter for one's family. Although that element of a house is very important, a person's home is also the receptacle for his or her dreams and often how a person defines him- or herself to the world. In fact, one of the reasons people do not look into bankruptcy sooner is a general belief that you lose your home when you file for bankruptcy.

This often does not happen, but it can. To avoid losing your home, planning on borrowing can be very important. Almost every state allows a person to keep his or her home if he or she does not have too much *equity* in the house (the value of the house less what is owed on it). How much equity you can have will vary by state. In New York, it is $50,000. In New Jersey, there is no state exemption, but one can use the federal exemption of $20,200. Some states—notably Florida and Texas—allow unlimited exemptions (but do limit the size of the property).

If you have equity in your home over the allowed maximum, you run the risk of losing your home. The trustee can sell it, give you the protected equity, and distribute the balance of sale proceeds to your creditors. The trustee will typically give you the chance to buy the house first at the price he or she would likely receive from the sale, but most people cannot normally come up with a large amount of money when filing for bankruptcy.

One way to avoid this problem is to have more debt on your home. Here is a place where it might make sense to borrow against your home in order to pay off your business and personal debts. If you can weather your financial storm by reducing your credit card payments, and move your house equity into the protected zone, this program of borrowing may make sense, but only in a planned, logical way. To do this, you need to know three things:

1. what the home exemption is in your state;

2. how much you owe on your home; and,

3. the value of your home.

Finding out the value of your home is not as simple as it seems. Most people, when asked for the value of their home, will give the value it was appraised at. Historically, this made sense, as banks wanted their appraisals to be concrete. Today, lenders are more interested in having the loan go through. To do this they need a good house value. The lending industry is now putting pressure on appraisers to *push* the house values—to give a house the highest plausible value.

The problem is that these artificially pushed values are often unrealistic when it comes to selling the house, particularly if the sale is to be soon after the appraisal. In your planning you might collect a realistic value for the house. Normally this is a blending of real estate agents' values (which are also often high), the appraisal value, and the tax value. It is well worth paying a bankruptcy lawyer to discuss with you what the local legal bankruptcy culture on house value is before making your borrowing plans. You may even want to hire your own appraiser and tell him or her to not artificially push the value. You are working with your most precious asset and you do not want to be flying blind when making your plans.

When you have these numbers, it makes sense to borrow up to the line of your state exemption, and no further. If your state exemption is $10,000 and your home has $30,000 in equity, borrow $20,000 against your home and pay down other bills. This way you may successfully overcome your financial problems.

Be Able to Pay Monthly Installments

Sometimes it makes sense to borrow against your house to pay back what you borrowed from your 401(k) or retirement plan. As previously noted, loans from retirement programs can hurt you in a bankruptcy, and loans against extra equity in your house, within limits, can help you save your home.

Within limits is a key phrase. It does not do you a bit of good to borrow against your home if you cannot make the monthly payments in full and on time. Whether it is called a *second mortgage* or a *home equity loan*, it still has your house as collateral. As such, you will lose your home to foreclosure if you do not make the monthly payments. (It is amazing how many business owners, when asked to list the mortgages against their home, will not list a home equity line. Somehow the difference in the name fools them.)

Borrowing from Family Members and Giving a Vehicle or Home as Security

After reviewing the problems of borrowing against a vehicle or a home, people often go to family and friends to borrow money instead. They give their car title or promise their home as security for the loan. The lender in such a friendly loan situation will either hold the car title or have his or her name listed as a lien holder on the title. If it is a loan against the home, the lender will draw up a note him- or herself and note that the home is the collateral for the loan. Such informal loans and security actions almost never hold up in bankruptcy court. The trustee sets aside the lender's claim and the vehicle or home is treated as if nothing was owed on it.

If someone is going to lend you money with your vehicle or home as security, take the time to put the transaction on a formal basis with the proper security documents. It is better to spend a little money to have a lawyer do the paperwork right than to possibly permanently alienate yourself from your friends or family. And remember, if the documents are not correct, your family member might have to give back the loan payments because it is considered an *insider preference*.

Taking a Cash Advance on a Credit Card

As money pressures mount, people often turn to whatever credit they can to gain funds to keep the business going and to live on. Common sources are credit cards, large cash advances, or cashing the checks creditors often send to people in the mail. The problem with taking cash advances is that this creates a spike in your borrowing pattern. There once was a time when if a creditor extended you credit and you were not able to repay it, that was the creditor's problem. But over the years, the credit card companies were able to convince courts that such debts should not be discharged.

Credit card companies started looking for anything that looked like a spending spree, such as a large charge in a short period of time. A large cash advance or cashing a mailed check will be treated as the same burst of spending as a Las Vegas vacation. Often the credit cards will attack first and try to put the burden on you to demonstrate you were not trying to defraud them. This aggressive action by the credit card industry when you take cash advances or cash checks can make your bankruptcy more expensive as you may have to defend yourself in bankruptcy court, and you may even lose if the judge does not think you acted properly. The best advice is not to change your charging habits.

Living on Credit Cards

If you are using a credit card to tide you over the rough spots, you should be reasonable. You must make a realistic assessment of when there is no hope of turning the business around, and when you need to go out and get another job. If it goes to court or is challenged by the credit card company, the judge will make an assessment of your judgment and whether you should have thought you had a realistic chance of repaying the money you were borrowing on the credit card.

Transferring Balances from One Card to Another

Sometimes advice you are given about trying to work yourself out of debt can come back to harm you. One bit of advice people often hear is to move debt from a high interest credit card to a lower interest credit card. This helps by reducing the amount you must pay each month, and in theory makes it easier to pay off your debts.

The problem with this strategy in the bankruptcy context is that it creates the same type of spike on the new lower interest credit card that a cash advance or a Las Vegas trip would. And even though the credit card company encouraged you to take this action in its promotional literature, it may turn around and attack you for bankruptcy fraud. You will be faced with the expense and worry of responding to these claims and accusations.

Again, the best safeguard against this type of problem is sober judgment. You must step back and make an assessment as to whether or not making such a balance transfer will really help or whether you are merely rearranging the deck chairs on the Titanic.

Lying or Exaggerating on Loan Applications

Bankruptcy has a way of making small lies about your income or your assets on loan applications blow up in your face. For large loans, you may have to produce income tax records, but often people are able to make a case that they are not accurate and have the loan officer accept the explanation. Or, the potential borrower may give insurance replacement value or more for business equipment and personal items. Often this is done with the acquiescence or even the prompting of the loan officer. One story heard fairly often is that a finance company loan person will tell the would-be borrower, "You don't have enough asset value to qualify for the loan. Think again about your goods and their value." Some even go through the application and systematically mark up the values given.

All of this blows up when a bankruptcy petition is filed. The income is lower and is not based on predictions but on cold, depressing facts. The values of goods and property are listed at a far lower forced-sale value. The relatively friendly and helpful loan officer disappears. In his or her place comes a stern recovery officer waving the loan application and implying fraud on the part of the borrower. These differences can be very hard to explain even if the difference is the innocent *puffing-up of numbers* when applying for the loan. The consequences can be far worse if you actually lied.

At best, loans made on the basis of your fraud are not dischargeable, and at worst, you may face criminal charges of fraud. Never lie on a loan application. Always try to put a fair value on your assets and do not let the loan officer put down information that is not correct. The same statements are always made: "I didn't say (or write) that," and then, "That's your signature, isn't it?" If you sign the document, it does not matter whether or not you wrote down the wrong price or not. By signing the document, you are saying that you agree with what is written on it at the time you sign.

Not Paying Income Taxes

When you are having money problems, a seemingly easy source of money is the government. People simply do not pay their taxes. It takes every bit of money they have to stay afloat, and at year-end they have nothing to send the government. Small business owners are particularly susceptible to this, as they do not have wages from which to withhold.

This is a big mistake. The Internal Revenue Service (IRS) may be acting nicer lately, but it is still a very hard organization to deal with. Taxes are a necessary, integral part of a business, and if you cannot afford to pay them, you should not be in business. It is possible to be opportunistic for a year and come up short at the end of the year, but the IRS will be much less sympathetic if you have several years of not paying your taxes.

File a tax return even if you cannot pay your taxes for the year or do not believe you owe any because of low income or losses.

In certain cases it is possible to completely discharge taxes in bankruptcy. The rules are complex, but basically the taxes must be old and you must have filed your tax returns. If you do not file your returns, you are not eligible for this limited chance at complete discharge.

When it comes time to deal with your late taxes, they will be much higher than the simple amount you owed for a given tax year. The IRS will add interest and penalties, which can be quite devastating.

Stopping Payment of Withholding

Closely allied to not paying your taxes is not paying money collected as sales taxes or as employee withholdings. Probably 75% of the businesses in financial trouble have taken this route. This is worse than not paying income tax. This type of tax liability cannot be discharged in bankruptcy. In addition, officers of the business are also liable for the taxes. This means if you made your wife or your daughter vice president or secretary, they will be personally liable even if they had nothing to do with the operation of the business.

Not Following Corporate Formalities

One of the reasons to establish a corporation is to protect your personal property, house, cars, savings, etc., from the claims of creditors. As previously noted, these assets are often at risk because business owners are forced to personally guarantee corporate debts.

But sometimes the corporate owner can avoid having his or her personal assets secure the business debts. This normally happens after the business has operated successfully for a few years. Lenders may stop requiring personal guarantees, and vendors may sell to the company and not the business owner. Then when the business slows down, these creditors have to start collection actions at once if they are to recover anything.

The organizers of the business are often careful to have the corporation formed and filed with the secretary of state. This is what breathes life into the corporation. They are typically less careful to take the steps to keep the corporation alive. To do this, you must mind the formalities of a corporation, and this means having meetings, authorizing corporate action, and electing officers. In some corporations, so little attention is paid to these formalities that organizational meetings are never held, thus creating a real question of whether or not the corporation was ever born. More common is to file with the state, hold the organizational meeting to elect directors and officers, and then put the corporate minutes book away and never take any of the actions necessary to keep the corporation alive.

This is a common temptation. You are busy running the corporation and you, or your small group of associates, are the corporation. You know what you are doing, you do it, and that is that. It is very unnatural to sit down, put on a shareholder's hat, elect directors, and then put on a director's hat, approve your business actions, and elect yourself as an officer. It seems like a silly formality at best. And what is worse, to be done correctly, it costs money to hire a lawyer to write up the documents. Keep in mind, though, that what seems like a silly formality can become all important when a business creditor is trying to take your house for a business debt.

How is this ever possible? The whole point of forming the corporation was to prevent such a thing from happening.

What the creditor will claim is that you did not have a real corporation—that the corporation is only your alter ego. You may have created the corporation, but you let it die from neglect and after a while the corporation no longer existed—it was just you or your group running the business as a sole proprietorship or a partnership. This is called *piercing the corporate veil*. Do not let this happen to you. If you went to the trouble and expense of forming the corporation, go to the extra expense and trouble of keeping it alive by taking corporate minutes as you go along.

If a collecting creditor is talking about piercing the corporate veil, do not go back and draw up several years of records at one time. You will open yourself up to charges of fraud. You are far better working your way through the facts you have than trying to create last minute changes.

ANALYZING BUSINESS DEBTS AND ASSETS BEFORE BANKRUPTCY | 10

As was noted in Section 5, it is very common for the small business owner to have large personal debts that are connected to or attributable to his or her business. Credit cards or personal loans may have been used to start the business or keep it going. Homes and vehicles may have been offered as security on these loans.

Business Debts

If you are considering bankruptcy for your business, you must determine how much personal liability you have for business debts. This discussion will apply only to business owners who have formed corporations or limited liability companies in an effort to shield their personal assets from business debts. If one is operating as a sole proprietor, then all business debts are personal debts. There are several classes of business debts discussed as follows.

Leases

Most businesses have a location where they operate. It may be a storefront where they sell goods or meet customers. Or, it may be a space where they repair items or perform other services. For most small businesses, this space is leased. Business owners typically think of this as an obligation of the business and believe that the lease will disappear if the business is shut down. This is often not true.

Most landlords know they will recover little or nothing for future missed rent payments if a business closes down. For this reason, most leases are written so that an individual personally guarantees the lease. To determine what you agreed to, carefully review your lease agreement to see if your name appears on the lease at the signature line. If it says the signer is "X Company by Tom Doe, President," or words to that effect, you may not have personally guaranteed the lease. However, if it merely has your name and your signature, you probably personally guaranteed the lease.

Vehicle and Equipment Leases

Vehicle and equipment leases will generally operate the same as real estate leases. Again, examine the document to see who the signing parties are.

Business Credit Cards

Today many business owners carry credit cards with their business name on them. Many people think these are business credit cards and that the money charged on them is the debt of the business only. This is often not correct. The agreement signed with the credit card company should be checked to see if it was signed by you as an officer of the company or by you individually.

Purchase Agreements

Businesses need supplies, and often these are bought on credit extended by the vendor. Sometimes vendors will set up the account in the name of the corporation or limited liability company, and sometimes they will set it up in your personal name. Most business owners do not pay attention to how vendors' accounts are set up when they are starting their business and when times are good. But this can make a big difference when times turn bad and the business owner must decide whether or not he or she will need to file bankruptcy and what debts should be listed.

If you do not have a copy of the vendor's contract, ask for one. Examine the contract to see who is listed as the contracting party. If there is not a formal contract, then examine the invoices sent to you. Often these will be used by the legal system to determine who the parties to the agreement are. Of course, all letters and memos between you and the vendor should be reviewed to see what light they can shed on who the parties to the credit extension are.

Another form of purchase agreement is when you have contracted to buy tools that you will need to use in your business. Often the sellers extend credit to buyers to allow the purchase of expensive tools and equipment. Normally, this credit is extended to the business owner as an individual, but the contracts should be read carefully.

Business Assets

Almost every business has assets, and often there is a great deal of confusion over whether or not a given asset is owned by the corporation or the individual. Some items, such as vehicles, are titled and it is a fairly straightforward matter to check the title to see who is listed as the owner. For other items it is harder. Computers, desks, typewriters, etc., are not titled and could belong to either the business or the individual. You should check tax records and maintenance agreements to see how they are listed. Also check the purchase agreements drawn up when you bought the item. Who is shown as the purchaser? Was a corporate or business check used to pay for the item? It is hard to argue that a computer is your personal property if it was paid for by a corporate check using corporate money, the warranty agreement is in the business's name, and it is listed as business property for tax purposes.

Value

Once you know who owns what, you should place a value on the property. If you file a personal bankruptcy, often what you lose or are allowed to keep will depend on the value of the goods. If the corporation owns the property and it files for bankruptcy, value does not matter because all corporate property will be taken.

Most people, when asked the value of their business or personal property, will list what they paid for it or what it would cost to replace the item. Sometimes they have no interest in selling the item and will place a higher value on the item since it would take that much money to induce them to sell it. Other times people will list what they would sell the item for if they had time and found just the right buyer. These are approaches that will lead to problems in most bankruptcies.

What the business owner should think about is how much the property would bring if it were sold in a fairly short period of time, or what one could get after making a reasonable effort to sell it. This should take into account the fact that the item is used and often not in the best shape. This is often the value to the bankruptcy system.

You should consider how easy it is to sell the item. Some things, like vehicles and baseball cards, have a ready market. Other items, such as collectibles, may bring a good price if you travel to another town to sell at a convention of collectors, but may bring almost nothing in your local town.

Vehicles are in a special class. There is a ready market for them and resale and market values are listed in books and on the Internet. Many people assume the value of a vehicle is what they can sell it for. This is not the case. The *value of a vehicle* is the value it would sell for at *retail* (from a car lot in the condition it is in).

Courts have come up with different ways of computing this value, which ranges from the full purchase price, to 90% of the purchase price, to an average of the retail values.

It is very hard for someone not used to dealing with the local bankruptcy court to come up with the value the court would use to value vehicles and other property.

The best course of action is to draw up a list of your assets, work out a sale value for them, and then talk to a lawyer to learn what value the court would use.

Profit and Loss

Most small business owners are in business because they have a skill they can sell or an activity they enjoy doing. Many, if not most, of them do not have any background in bookkeeping and do not enjoy doing it. In fact, many avoid it because time spent keeping the books is time away from making money. At best, they turn the recordkeeping over to a spouse or hired bookkeeper.

The result can be chaos. Many small business owners, when asked for income, will give what the business on average earns or clears each month, without taking taxes into account. Taxes are something paid at the end of the year and are to be worried about then. Gas for vehicles is lumped in with gas for personal cars. The same problem comes up with food if their business involves overnight travel.

This approach to business and personal debts has been called the *cigar box method* of running a business. In the past, a business owner kept a cigar box of cash by the cash register. When a sale was made, the money went into the box. When a supplier needed to be paid, the money came from the box. If money was needed for groceries, it came out of the box. Everything was fine as long as the box contained money, and no effort was made to differentiate between business expenses and personal expenses.

This will not work if you go into bankruptcy. Since bankruptcy is a personal matter, it is important to know how much the business is earning and what its expenses are, including taxes. When these are worked out, an individual can see what he or she has available for business expenses and can then work out what his or her personal living expenses are. Many small business owners are shocked to learn how little they are being paid for their long hours of hard work when they figure out their income and expenses.

TAKING A FINANCIAL INVENTORY | 11

There are two steps to taking a financial inventory. The first is seeing how bad your debt situation really is. The second is classifying your debts and assets.

Computing Your Debt Ratio

After interviewing thousands of people over the years, we have developed a quick test to determine just how bad a person's debt situation is. For lack of a better name, we call it the *Quick Ratio*. It is the relationship between your take-home pay and how much you owe, not counting your vehicle and house debt.

To work out your ratio, do the following (using the worksheet on page 84):

1. Take your paychecks and work out how much money you have each month after taxes, insurance, and retirement costs are deducted. Money your employer is withholding for payments to a credit union for an unsecured debt and money you are putting into savings (for stock purchases, a Christmas Club, etc.) need to be added back in. This gives you your *net pay*.

   If you and your spouse both work, compute net pay for both of you.

2. Multiply your monthly net pay by twelve to get your yearly take home income.

3. Add up the total of all your debts except what you owe on your house, vehicles, student loans, and taxes.

4. Divide your total short-term debt by your yearly income.

Quick Ratio Worksheet

1) My take home pay is _____

2) Add back:

    a) Holiday account _____

    b) Payment to credit union for signature loans _____

    c) Money to savings account _____

    d) Stock purchase _____

    e) Savings program _____

        Total _____

3) If you are paying spousal support, child support, or criminal restitution out of your take home pay, deduct these amounts _____

4) a) If you are paid weekly, multiply by 4.3 _____

    b) If you are paid every 2 weeks, multiply by 2.15 _____

    c) If you are paid 2 times a month, multiply by 2 _____

    d) If you are paid monthly, multiply by 1 _____

    Multiply your monthly income by 12 _____

5) My total short term debt (the actual debt; not just what you are paying each month) _____

a) Medical bills   _____

b) Money owed after repossessions   _____

c) Credit cards   _____

d) Bank loans   _____

e) Department store debt   _____

f) Finance company loans   _____

g) Jewelry debt   _____

h) Stereo and appliance debt   _____

i) Loans from family and friends   _____

    Total   _____

6) Total from step 5   _____

Divide by total from step 4   _____

Quick Ratio   _____

This quick test assumes you do not have unusually high housing, car, tax, or student loan payments. It also assumes your medical expenses and gifts to your religious institution are average. To get a very detailed debt to income ratio, all of these factors would need to be considered. But the Quick Ratio will give you a good starting point.

What the ratio means:

- If the ratio is .15 or lower, you are generally in good financial shape.

- If the ratio is .15 to .25, you are starting to get a little too much debt. You should cut back your spending and pay down your debt.

- If your Quick Ratio is over .25, you are showing signs of a dangerous debt situation. The larger the Quick Ratio, the worse your situation (of course, if your ratio is .26 you can fix things easier than if it is .65).

Generally speaking, people or couples whose ratio is between .35 and .85 are sinking deeper and deeper into debt. They may be able to make their minimum payments, but they are not taking care of the underlying debt. Even worse, they are slowly getting worse off. That is, if they add up their total debt from six months ago and their total debt today, today's debt is likely to be higher. Further, without some drastic action, the total debt six months in the future will be higher than it is today. Many people in this situation do not really realize the danger they are in and even think they have perfect credit. They are probably getting preapproved credit applications in the mail.

However, people with this ratio are slowly sinking into debt. The fact that their total debt is getting larger means that they are in effect paying the monthly payments on their debt with borrowed money when all is said and done. As long as they can get borrowed money from their credit cards or other creditors, they can easily make timely payments. But, this cannot go on forever. Eventually even the most foolish creditors will stop making money available. Without more money to help live and pay the monthly payments, it becomes impossible to stay afloat and a financial crisis occurs.

People with a Quick Ratio above .9 are very close to a financial crisis, if they are not already experiencing one.

There are two ways to get a high Quick Ratio. One is to borrow a lot of money either slowly or all at once. This increases the debt part of the equation. The other is to have a drop in personal or household income. This reduces the income part of the equation. If your household income is cut in half, you can go from a safe Quick Ratio to a very bad one overnight.

What should you do if your Quick Ratio is over .9? Make an appointment at once with a bankruptcy lawyer or call Consumer Credit Counseling. The phone number for Consumer Credit Counseling is listed in the business white pages of most phone books, or you can refer to Appendix C. You can also call the lawyer referral line of your state bar for a bankruptcy lawyer near you, or you can search on the Internet.

Classifying Your Debts and Assets

If your debt ratio is high, you should begin working out your mix of debts and assets in case you need to file bankruptcy. To gain a rough idea of how bankruptcy will affect you, you must first list and categorize your debts and assets. The bankruptcy court treats different debts in different ways; likewise, certain classes of assets are given different treatment.

Debts

At its simplest, a *debt* is a promise to pay someone a sum of money. However, in the modern world, this simple rule has been stretched and bent until a large number of items that are classified as debts must be dealt with in bankruptcy. The two main divisions are: (1) secured debts versus unsecured debts; and, (2) contingent debts versus present debts.

Secured debts. A *secured debt* is one where property can be taken by the creditor if the debt is not paid. The classic examples are car and house loans. If you do not pay these debts, the creditor can repossess your car or foreclose on your home. These simple concepts can be tricky. A surprising number of people feel that loans from finance companies where the finance company holds the car title are not secured car loans. They feel that since they paid off the original financing of the purchase of the car arranged with the dealer and the bank, they do not have a car loan anymore. A loan from a finance company that holds your car title is almost always a secured loan, and the company can repossess your car just as fast as the bank that did the original financing.

Likewise, many people do not consider home equity loans or lines of credit secured by a home to be mortgages. These are both secured by the home, and if they are not paid in a timely way the holder can foreclose on the home.

Jewelry or electronics bought with the selling company's credit card are often secured. A merchant company's credit card often has clauses in the contract that make it different from a true credit card. But, because they are both plastic and the same shape, people often believe both are unsecured credit card debts. Business owners often secure loans from creditors with company assets, inventory, equipment, and tools.

Unsecured debts. *Unsecured debts* are, by definition, debts without property pledged as security for the repayment of the debt. Examples are major credit cards such as Visa®, Master Card®, and American Express®. Medical debts, signature loans, and utility bills are other examples of unsecured debts. If you owe money on a car that has been repossessed and sold, that debt is unsecured—there is nothing more the lender can take from you.

Some credit card companies send credit solicitations to small business owners with offers for *company credit cards* or *business account cards*. When issued, the business name is written in large letters on the cards. Credit card companies offer the chance to charge business expenses on the card. Often they tout the value of having all your business expenses listed on one account for ease of record keeping. They may even list the advantage of earning free travel miles on your charges. The implication is that you can earn travel mileage points for

airline travel on tax-deductible business expenses. Some also stress that you can use their card for working capital.

Many business owners naturally think charges on these cards are company debts and that they are not personally responsible for the charges on the cards. This can be a serious mistake. You should closely examine the solicitation form you filled out and sent in when you signed up for the card (or the signature portion of the solicitation you are considering signing up for). Most of the time, the application will ask for your individual signature and your Social Security number. These are indications that they are issuing the card to you as an individual. They need your Social Security number to check your credit history before deciding whether or not to issue you the individual credit card. The company name on the card is merely to appeal to your ego and what little advantage you get in record keeping and earning travel miles on business expenses. The emphasis behind it is in marketing cards via affinity, the way clubs and colleges have an affinity card. Money owed on these business credit cards should be counted as personal unsecured debt when you are taking your financial inventory.

Sometimes debts that appear secured are treated as unsecured in bankruptcy. Often finance companies, when they make you a loan, have you list property you already own as security—televisions, furniture, etc. In bankruptcy, these *non-purchase security items* can often be protected by filing a special motion. The test is: are they items you already owned and used to operate your household? What is considered a *household good* will vary from state to state. Often sports equipment, such as golf clubs or tennis rackets, is not considered necessary to operate a household and does not fall within this exemption. Firearms are treated differently from state to state.

Contingent debts. *Contingent debts* are those that are dependent on an event that has not yet happened. A straightforward example is being a codebtor on a loan. You will not owe the money unless the main borrower defaults. Another type is the so-called *unliquidated debt*. This is when you may or may not owe the debt. This normally arises in a car accident where you are being sued by a person who says the accident and the damages were your fault. You dispute this claim. You do not owe him or her anything until the court rules against you and sets a dollar amount you are to pay.

Other debt types. There are several other types of debts covered on bankruptcy forms.

- **Unmatured debts.** These are debts in which the event creating the duty to pay has not yet occurred. For example, you borrowed money and gave a promise to pay it back in three years. Until those three years have passed, you have only future liability and the debt is unmatured. After the three years have passed, the debt becomes matured. This is a form of contingent debt.

- **Disputed debts.** This is another form of contingent debt. This is a debt a third party claims you owe him or her, but that you deny. There are several situations where this can arise. You hire someone to do work for you and he or she does a bad job. He or she claims payment and you deny you owe him or her that much because of the poor quality of the work. Another common situation is where you have paid the debt and the creditor claims he or she never received the money. The creditor may still be trying to collect, or the claim may only be on your credit report. Another situation is where you never bought anything from the creditor, but he or she claims you owe money and is trying to collect on it or is listing it on your credit report.

- **Cosigned debts.** Some debts are debts where you and another person have both signed for a loan. You are both liable. It does not make any difference whose name is first on the loan. You are each liable for the entire debt. Many people believe that since there are two or three signers, they are only liable for one-half or one-third of the debt. This is not true. Each person can be sued for the entire debt. Whom the company goes after for the money is completely up to the creditor.

Taxes, student loans, spousal support, child support, and criminal fines.

Debts are also classified by to whom the money is owed. The most common are taxes, student loans, spousal support, child support, and criminal fines.

- **Taxes.** These are debts owed to a government entity—federal, state, or local. These debts may or may not be dischargeable depending on the type of tax and how old it is. Some taxes cannot be discharged in bankruptcy at all. Two examples are withholding taxes and sales taxes. Back income taxes may be discharged if they are old enough and certain other conditions are met.

- **Student loans.** At one time, student loans, if they were old enough, could be discharged in bankruptcy. Congress has ended this exemption. Now, except for cases of *extreme hardship*, student loans cannot be wiped out in bankruptcy. Owing a lot of money and having no funds is not extreme hardship. This is the situation of almost everyone in the bankruptcy courts. What is extreme hardship is decided by a judge in each case, so results vary. It often involves a new sickness or disability that would prevent you from ever making the income necessary to repay the loan.

- **Spousal support.** Occasionally people come to us with the bright idea of wiping out their duty to pay spousal support in bankruptcy. It cannot be done. In fact, spousal support is so protected in the bankruptcy procedure that some regular debts are deemed spousal support and are protected from bankruptcy discharge. Often in the past, a person, in separation or divorce papers, would agree to pay certain debts owed by both spouses. Many times this was in exchange for not paying spousal support. The trade-off was, "I will pay the debts so I cannot afford to pay spousal support." The person would then file bankruptcy and thus end up without spousal support or debts. The ex-spouse would end up with no spousal support and would be liable on the joint debts.

Congress put a stop to this by saying that such debts were to be treated as a form of spousal support and cannot be discharged if the spouse objects to the debt being wiped out. This system does not prevent a person from trying to wipe out these debts and puts the burden on the spouse to object.

- **Child support.** Just like spousal support, this simply cannot be wiped out in bankruptcy.

- **Criminal fines and court-ordered restitution.** These cannot be wiped out in bankruptcy. In fact, the bankruptcy court has remarkably little power to interfere with what a criminal court is doing.

Assets

Home. The average person's most important asset is his or her home, both in monetary value and in psychological terms. The biggest worry people always have is, "Will I lose my home?" Normally they will not. If you look at the exemption charts in Appendix B, you will see that the value of a home that can be protected is normally quite small. Ten to thirty thousand dollars is the normal range. However, this is *equity value*, the difference between the *market value* (what you could sell it for) and what is owed on it in first, second, and third mortgages. As long as your home equity is within the protected range, your home is safe.

There are three things to keep in mind when you are determining equity value.

1. Many people have trouble determining the market value of their home. They first, naturally enough, give the value the appraiser used for the mortgage on their home. Unfortunately this is not always a true market value. Many lenders are now putting pressure on appraisers to *push* the appraised value. That is, they want appraisers to give an appraisal figure that is the highest supportable value.

The higher the appraisal, the more likely the loan will go through. After all, lenders do not make money, and their employees do not earn salaries, unless loans are made. It may be that the mortgage industry is gambling that it will never have to try to recoup loaned money by actually selling the homes that secure loans.

Since you cannot depend on the appraised value, estimates and averages are the next best thing. Many areas are using tax value. Historically, tax values of homes were lower than the true market value of the property. That is not always the case today. Some taxing authorities have found they can raise more taxes by having a higher tax appraisal on the homes and other property in its jurisdiction. People generally like being told their homes are worth more, and those who object to the increased value (and the higher taxes it produces) are often too busy to go through the laborious process of protesting the higher assessed value. Thus over time, tax value has moved closer to actual value.

2. Another source of information is a real estate agent. It may be possible to have a real estate agent give you an idea of what your house would sell for. Just be aware that many real estate people are by nature optimistic. They may also push the value of the house to some degree.

3. If in doubt, you can always pay to have an appraisal done by your own appraiser. This is not foolproof. The appraiser can be wrong about the value. Some people think they will hire a friendly appraiser and get a low value appraisal for their home. This is a mistake.

    A trustee can question the appraiser's value, leading to a trial and great expense. But having a fair appraisal does give you another source of information about your most valuable asset.

The bigger problem comes when a home does not have a mortgage on it, either because the mortgage has been paid off (as often happens with older people) or because the mortgage is no good. This does not happen often, but occasionally the mortgage will have a technical flaw. The description of the property may be wrong, it may be recorded in the wrong county, or even not properly signed.

If any of these things happen, the value of the asset is likely to be far higher than the relatively low protection value for homes allowed by most states.

Other real estate. This category can cover vacation homes, time shares, and investment property (such as rental homes, second homes, and homes owned for family members to live in). This property, not being the place where the filer actually lives, is generally not protected by federal or state exemptions.

Vehicles. These can be either personal or company cars. As with houses, the exemption for these in most states is quite low. Therefore, if the vehicle is owned outright and is fairly new, it may be lost in bankruptcy.

People are often surprised by how high the value is on their vehicles in the bankruptcy system. When they seek to sell the vehicle or to borrow money against it, they are faced with a far lower value. The reason for this difference is that in bankruptcy, the value is *retail value*. Thus the courts look to see what a dealer would charge you if you bought the vehicle from its lot.

Rented or leased personal property. Leased property, vehicle leases, or rent-to-own property, such as televisions, stereo systems, and furniture, are not uncommon. The right to use the property is an asset, but is normally not one that would be lost in bankruptcy.

Personal household goods. *Personal household goods* include items such as furniture, clothes, jewelry, books, musical instruments, etc. This is the most elastic classification of them all. Different state laws, and the federal bankruptcy laws where applicable, will protect various classes of these goods in different ways. What can be protected and up to what limit varies greatly state-by-state. To gain a rough idea of what you may be able to protect, you should refer first to Appendix B on exemptions.

But be aware that this will only give you a rough idea. Each locale has different nuances to its exemptions. One locale may not treat golf clubs or fishing equipment as household goods. Pistols and rifles may or may not be treated as household goods. A pistol for home protection may be a household item, but a rifle that is used for hunting may not be. Iowa, for example, traditionally allows you to keep a rifle or shotgun.

Items may move from one category to another depending on how they are used. Artwork hung on the wall can be a household item, but several drawings stacked up in a storage area may be classified as investment property rather than a household item. Your best guide is a lawyer who is aware of the local treatment of different items.

The lawyer will also be your best guide to evaluation. People's natural tendency is to value property at replacement value, or to give the price they paid for the item. But the court system may require you to value the items at pawnshop value or some other value that is significantly below what you paid for it.

Often the court system will not push too hard on items such as furniture, appliances, and clothing. These are relatively low-value items, and as a practical matter the trustee would lose money if he or she tried to take them and sell them to raise funds to pay creditors. The time spent would be worth more than the relatively small amounts the items would bring at an auction.

The story is quite different for other items with a ready, identifiable market and resale value. Jewelry, silver, baseball cards, and other collections may have high value and be relatively easy for the trustee to sell.

Tools. Tools can generally be divided into two types: those used for hobby purposes and those used for business or work (*tools of trade*). Hobby tools would have to be protected under household goods, if they could be protected at all.

Tools of trade are items you use to make a living and they are what are most likely to apply to you as a business operator. These can vary. New Hampshire allows you one yoke of oxen used for teaming, Nevada allows a cabin for mining and a mining claim, and the District of Columbia protects the seal and documents of a notary public. Almost all have a catch-all rule for tools and books. Once again, valuation is very important. Most people's first instinct is to value the tools at what they paid for them. The better course is to value them at what they would bring in if you sold them in a short period of time or in a pawnshop.

In some states, the level of protection can be depressingly low. This often presents a hard choice to the person contemplating a bankruptcy filing. If you will lose your tools or books if you file a Chapter 7 bankruptcy, you are out of business and cannot earn a livelihood. A lawyer is not much good without his or her law books and computers, and a mechanic is not much good without his or her wrenches. It is the need to keep the tools and equipment that causes many small business owners to consider a Chapter 13 bankruptcy, even if they qualify for Chapter 7.

Other items of personal property. There is a vast number of items that do not fall into the categories of vehicles, household goods, and business tools. Depending on the state, these may or may not be protected. Examples of items that are protected are: church pews (Delaware), articles of adornment (Colorado), athletic and sporting equipment (Texas), and required arms and uniforms (Nevada).

Generally, items such as tanning beds, boats, campers, etc., will be hard to keep, but the levels of protected goods are so varied from state to state that you should always check with a lawyer before making your plans.

Retirement savings. You may have carefully saved money for retirement over the years. Generally, as long as the retirement program (company pension plan, IRA, 401(k), etc.) is ERISA qualified, it will be protected. (*ERISA* is a federal law that regulates retirement plans.) Most pension programs are protected. Occasionally, small business owners make mistakes in how they manage their retirement money and move outside the protected zone. So for example, if you are the trustee of your company's retirement program, do not give the money to your brother-in-law to invest in a trailer park or to operate a rabbit ranch.

Leased equipment. This is often a major category for the small business owner. Often the business depends on leased equipment to operate, from restaurants to dentist offices. The right to use the equipment is a property right, but it is useless if you cannot make the lease payments. The bankruptcy trustee is normally not all that interested in taking leased equipment, as he or she cannot sell it (it belongs to the lessor). This often allows the business owner a choice to keep the business going. If the business can keep operating and generating enough funds to pay the lease payments, then the business has a chance of surviving.

Accounts receivable. Often businesses or business owners have accounts receivable, which they have not been able to collect or which are simply outstanding. One of the factors that brings on financial problems for small business owners is not being able to collect on accounts receivable. In taking your financial inventory, you should classify these accounts into likely collectible, possible, and bad debts. If you should have to file bankruptcy, the trustee will want an assessment of how likely it is that a given accounts receivable can be collected.

What Will I Lose?

There is a widespread belief that you will lose all your property if you file bankruptcy. This is often not the case. There are ways to predict what you might lose and how to make an assessment of what is at risk.

What is protected in bankruptcy and what is lost will depend in large part on what state you live in. Appendix B gives a state-by-state breakdown of the levels of protection.

In looking to see what will be lost in bankruptcy, remember that after you file, two sets of people have an interest in your property. First, there is the *trustee*, whose duty is to collect property that is not exempt and sell it for the benefit of your creditors. The state exemptions set out what is *exempt* or protected from the trustee. The second group is the *secured creditors*. These are entities such as mortgage holders on your home or lienholders on your cars and trucks. If they are not paid they can repossess your home or vehicle. Often a trustee will not be interested in the property because more is owed on it than it is worth. This means the trustee would not make any money from the general creditors if the property was seized and sold. So the trustee does not usually bother with the property.

Let's take two small business owners—Sue and Tom—and see how they would be treated in three different states: North Carolina, Texas, and Ohio.

Example 1: Sue

Sue has been careful in starting her business and has limited what she has bought over the years. She has one child, age 10, who loves to ride horses. Her one luxury is a horse for the child to ride after school and on weekends. Sue has debts of $70,000, which are a mix of business and personal debts, and has the following property.

Property	Equity
1. A home with a market value of $100,000. The first and second mortgages total $102,000.	– $2,000 ($100,000 – $102,000)
2. An SUV worth $26,000. She owes $27,000 on it.	– $1,000 ($26,000 – $27,000)
3. A second vehicle worth $3,000.	$3,000
4. Tools and equipment used in her business worth $2,000.	$2,000
5. Household furnishings and clothes worth $4,000.	$4,000
6. A 401(k) plan with $50,000 in stocks.	$50,000
7. A horse worth $1,500.	$1,500

North Carolina

The applicable property values that are exempted in North Carolina are as follows.

1. Home equity	$18,500
2. Car equity (for 1 vehicle)	$3,500

3. Work tools and equipment $2,000

4. Household goods $5,000

5. Extra protection for household
    goods for each dependent $1,000

6. A wild card of up to $5,000 for the home
    equity not already exempted. (A *wild card*
    can be used to protect anything.) $5,000

In North Carolina, Sue will have her property treated as follows.

1. Home	**Sue can keep:** *There is $0 equity in the home, so the trustee will not take it to sell for the benefit of the creditors. Sue will need to continue paying the first and second mortgages, though, to protect the home from the mortgage holders.*
2. SUV	**Sue can keep:** *There is $0 equity in the SUV, so the trustee will not take it to sell for the benefit of the creditors. Sue will need to continue to pay the lienholder to protect the SUV, though.*
3. Second vehicle	**Exempt:** *The second car is worth $3,000. The $3,500 vehicle protection can be applied against this vehicle.*
4. Work tools and equipment	**Exempt:** *They are worth $2,000. The $2,000 is protected by the work tool exemption.*
5. Household goods	**Exempt:** *Sue's household goods are worth $4,000. She can protect $5,000 worth of household goods, and even if this was not enough, she can protect an additional $1,000 worth of household goods on behalf of her daughter.*
6. Stocks in 401(k)	**Exempt:** *All the money in a pension plan is protected by the Bankruptcy Code.*
7. Horse	**Exempt:** *Sue can use $1,500 of her remaining wild card exemption to protect the value of her horse.*

Texas

In Texas, the property values that fall under the exemption are as follows.

1. Home equity	Unlimited: There is no limit on the value of a homestead, but there is a limit on the number of acres.
2. Miscellaneous	The head of the household can protect home furnishings, clothes, one motor vehicle, tools of trade, and two horses, as long as the total value is less than $60,000.

In Texas, Sue will have her property treated as follows.

1. Home	**Sue can keep:** *There is $0 equity in the home, so the trustee will not take it to sell for the benefit of the creditors. Sue will need to continue paying the first and second mortgages, though, to protect the home from the mortgage holders.*
2. SUV	**Sue can keep:** *There is $0 equity in the SUV, so the trustee will not take it to sell for the benefit of the creditors. Sue will need to continue to pay the lienholder to protect the SUV, though.*
3. Second vehicle	**Exempt:** *Sue can use her one vehicle protection for her second car as part of her general $60,000 exemption.*
4. Work tools and equipment	**Exempt:** *This is part of her $60,000 exemption.*
5. Household goods	**Exempt:** *This is part of her $60,000 exemption.*
6. Stocks in 401(k)	**Exempt:** *All the money in a pension plan is protected by the Bankruptcy Code.*
7. Horse	**Exempt:** *Up to two horses can be protected as part of her $60,000 exemption.*

Ohio

In Ohio, the applicable property values that can be protected are as follows.

1. Home equity $5,000

2. Vehicle equity $1,000

3. Work tools and equipment $750

4. Household goods A person has a general $2,000 exemption, which can be used to protect the filer's property. However, the exemption drops to $1,500 if a homestead exemption is claimed. Clothes are protected.

The result for Sue in Ohio is as follows.

1. Home	**Sue can keep:** *There is $0 equity in the home, so the trustee will not take it to sell for the benefit of the creditors. Sue will need to continue paying the first and second mortgages, though, to protect the home from the mortgage holders.*
2. SUV	**Sue can keep:** *There is $0 equity in the SUV, so the trustee will not take it to sell for the benefit of the creditors. Sue will need to continue to pay the lienholder to protect the SUV, though.*
3. Second vehicle	**$1,000 of the $3,000 value is exempt.**
4. Work tools and equipment	**$750 of the $2,000 value is exempt.**
5. Household goods	**$2,000 of the household furnishings is exempt. All clothes are exempt.**
6. Stocks in 401(k)	**Exempt:** *All the money in a pension plan is protected by the Bankruptcy Code.*
7. Horse	**Not Exempt.**

Example 2: Tom

Tom has spent more than Sue in running his business and owns property worth more than Sue's property. Tom also has one child, age 10, who loves to ride horses. His one luxury is a horse for the child to ride after school and on the weekends. Tom has debts of $140,000, and has the following property:

Property	Equity
1. A home with a market value of $200,000. The first and second mortgages total $45,000.	$155,000 ($200,000 – $45,000)
2. An SUV worth $26,000. He owes $16,000 on it.	$10,000 ($26,000 – $16,000)
3. A second vehicle worth $3,000.	$3,000
4. Tools and equipment used in his business worth $4,000.	$4,000
5. Household furnishings and clothes worth $8,000.	$8,000
6. A 401(k) plan with $100,000 in stocks.	$100,000
7. A horse worth $3,000.	$3,000

North Carolina

In North Carolina, Tom will have his property treated as follows.

1. Home	**Not fully exempt.** *Tom will be able to exempt only $18,500 of the $155,000 he has in equity on the home.*
2. SUV	**Not exempt.** *The $10,000 in equity is larger than the $3,500 vehicle exemption. He cannot protect this much equity even if the wild card was added to it.*
3. Second vehicle	**Exempt:** *The $3,500 vehicle exemption can be applied to this car.*
4. Work tools and equipment	**Exempt:** *The first $2,000 of equity in the tools falls under the work tool exemption. Tom can protect the remaining $2,000 through the wild card exemption.*
5. Household goods	**Exempt:** *Tom can protect the first $5,000 worth of household goods as the head of the household, and the next $1,000 worth of household goods can be protected on behalf of his child. The remaining $2,000 worth of equity can be protected using the wild card exemption.*
6. Stocks in 401(k)	**Exempt:** *All the money in a pension plan is protected by the Bankruptcy Code.*
7. Horse	**Not fully exempt.** *Tom can use $1,000 of his remaining wild card to protect part of the value of the horse.*

Texas

In Texas, Tom will have his property treated as follows.

1. Home	**Exempt:** *There is no dollar limit on home value—only an acre limit.*
2. SUV	**Exempt:** *This is part of his $60,000 exemption.*
3. Second vehicle	**Not exempt:** *Tom can only protect one vehicle.*
4. Work tools and equipment	**Exempt:** *This is part of his $60,000 exemption.*
5. Household goods	**Exempt:** *This is part of his $60,000 exemption.*
6. Stocks in 401(k)	**Exempt:** *All the money in a pension plan is protected by the Bankruptcy Code.*
7. Horse	**Exempt:** *This is part of his $60,000 exemption.*

Ohio

The result for Tom in Ohio is as follows.

1. Home	**$5,000 of the value of the home is exempt.**
2. SUV	**$1,000 of the value of the SUV is exempt.**
3. Second vehicle	**Not exempt.**
4. Work tools and equipment	**$750 of the value of the work tools is exempt.**
5. Household goods	**All of his clothes, and $2,000 worth of household furnishings** (*$1,500 worth of household furnishings if he uses the home equity exemption*)
6. Stocks in 401(k)	**Exempt:** *All the money in a pension plan is protected by the Bankruptcy Code.*
7. Horse	**Not Protected.**

Observations

A few observations are in order. The result of what was exempt and what was not did not depend on the size of the unsecured debt. However, it did vary depending on the amount of secured debt that there was against homes and vehicles. From this example, Texas is clearly the best place to live if you have to file for bankruptcy, and Ohio is the worst place to have to file.

Texas and Ohio are extreme examples. Most states fall somewhere in between. Each state varies greatly in how it treats different items of property and in what dollar limits it places on each class of property. However, in most states you increase your likelihood of losing property if you have assets, such as vehicles and homes, that are almost paid off.

People who live in states with low zones of protection have the option of filing a Chapter 13 bankruptcy. If they file a Chapter 13 bankruptcy, they will have to pay `at least what the creditors would have received in a Chapter 7 bankruptcy, but they have several years to accomplish this.

DOS AND DON'TS OF FILING FOR BANKRUPTCY

When a small business owner starts to realize that bankruptcy is a real possibility, he or she will begin to think of steps that he or she can take to protect his or her hard-earned property for his or her family. Some of these steps will merely cause problems when and if bankruptcy is filed, while others may consist of fraud and cause the person to end up in jail.

Common steps people consider are:

- paying themselves bonuses after not receiving a salary;

- taking goods from the business;

- paying off loans to family members and close friends;

- transferring or selling property to family or friends at a low price;

- paying off car loans;

- buying a new car; and,

- hiding assets.

Paying Themselves a Bonus After Not Receiving a Salary

When a business begins to have cash flow problems, most entrepreneurs will reduce their draws or stop paying themselves altogether. Then when it looks like the business may have to be bankrupted, they start thinking about the extra money in the corporate bank account, and how they have not been paid for their very hard work. There is a strong temptation to pay themselves a bonus or to pay off the loans to themselves they put on the company books when they did not draw a salary.

Do not do this. When the corporation goes into a Chapter 7 bankruptcy (a corporation cannot file a Chapter 13), the trustee is likely to view this as fraud and at the very least force you to pay the money back to the corporation. Remember, a corporation is a separate legal entity and you have a special relationship to it. You cannot use your power over the corporation as the proprietor in charge to take money out to pay one creditor (yourself) or to pay management (yourself). To do so runs the risk of adding to your money problems. Every year, people go to jail for bankruptcy fraud.

The problem is similar even if you are not incorporated. If you are not incorporated, the temptation to pay money to yourself out of the business bank account will be much smaller as the business creditors will also be your personal creditors. This means that all you are doing by moving money from a business account to your personal account is moving money from one pocket to the other. The creditors can still get to the money whether it is in your personal bank account or in the business bank account.

Taking Goods from the Business

Closely allied with taking money out of the business is the practice of taking tools and equipment from a business that is about to go under. This is a special temptation when you have small mobile items such as Palm Pilots or laptop computers. These items are not titled, will have little liquidation value to the business, and may be expensive to buy if you have to buy them new. Software falls into the same category. People tend to see such takings as little white thefts, if they think of them as thefts at all. But again, to remove items that the corporation paid for prior to bankruptcy is bankruptcy fraud.

Paying Off Loans to Family Members and Close Friends

Payments to family members are specifically forbidden by the bankruptcy code. In fact, any payment to insiders, such as family, within the two-year period proceeding filing for bankruptcy can be recaptured by the trustee. This is clearly true if you make a last minute repayment of loans to the business as a lump sum.

But this can also trap you when you have a practice of making monthly payments to your family members for a loan they made to you. Let us say you borrowed $10,000 from your parents one year ago. Since then you have paid $500 back to them each month as a loan repayment—a total of $6,000 has been paid to them. The trustee can go to your parents and take the $6,000 to pay it to other creditors.

The terrible part of this trap is that people often borrow against their houses or retirement accounts to make the loan in the first place. They do not have the $6,000 to pay back to the trustee, and if their child cannot pay them back, they risk losing their home or a large part of their retirement.

Since repayments to parents can have such negative consequences, you should never borrow money from family members when it is money they cannot afford to simply write off. Borrowing from your family to fund the start-up of your business, or to get you out of financial trouble when your business hits a downturn, may seem like a good idea. Your family will lend to you when no one else will. However, in reality it is a terrible trap if they cannot afford to write off any money they lent to you and you are forced to declare bankruptcy within two years of accepting a loan from them.

Transferring or Selling Property to Family or Friends at a Low Price

Another temptation when considering bankruptcy is to sell or transfer goods to family members. When people begin to realize the limited scope of property that can be protected after filing for bankruptcy, their first thought is to simply get the property out of their name. This is often done with noble interest. For example, a child's car may have been put in his or her parents' name for insurance purposes, or because the child could not qualify for the loan when it was purchased. Everyone knows it was the child's car because he or she paid for it, but somehow it was never put in his or her name. When the parents file bankruptcy, since the car title is in the parents' name, it is considered to be their property and subject to being taken by the bankruptcy court. Often debtors feel it is unfair that the child will lose his or her car because of a legal technicality. Thus people want to transfer the car title to the child where they think it really should be.

Bankruptcy is a maze of technicalities and steps to fix the legalities. The facts as you and your family understand them can rapidly lead to large problems in bankruptcy. The sale of property for too low a price to a family member or a friend, or simply giving it to someone, can lead both you and the other party into real trouble. The bankruptcy forms ask about such transactions and you will be faced with the decision to tell about them or to lie.

To tell the truth will cause the transaction to be undone, and will likely cause heightened review of your whole case by the trustee. If you lie, you have committed bankruptcy fraud and you expose yourself to a criminal conviction for a federal crime. It is far better to work your way through the bankruptcy with the facts as you have them when you started having money problems.

Paying Off Car Loans

Cars and what to do about them are also a fruitful source of missteps for people who are having money problems. After a little research or after asking around, many people come to the understanding that the bankruptcy laws allow them to keep a car. So they pay off their car shortly before seeing a lawyer, or they may have made a point of making their car payments all along and now own their car free and clear.

This can potentially be as bad as having too much equity in your house. Take a look at your state's exemption for a motor vehicle. You will be shocked. Most exemptions are in the $2,000–$4,000 range, and you have to use retail value to determine the value of your vehicle. If the car has a value above your state's exemption, then you must either give the car up—and receive back money equal to the state exemption when it is sold—or pay the difference, assuming you can raise the money to pay the difference. You are, in effect, paying for the vehicle twice—once when you paid for it and a second time to the trustee to keep it.

It is far better to owe money on your car, as this will reduce the value of the car. Say you have a vehicle worth $10,000. If you own it free and clear, you will have to pay an amount equal to $10,000 less your state exemption. However, if you owed $9,000 on the car, it would only have a value of $1,000, which is probably within your state's protected zone for vehicles, and you would not have to pay anything to the trustee. (Of course, you will still need to pay the vehicle's lienholder or the lienholder can take the vehicle.)

Buying a New Car

The mirror image of having a fairly new car that is paid for can present a trap in bankruptcy. When someone with an old, unreliable car starts to have financial problems and considers bankruptcy, he or she may realize that once he or she files for bankruptcy, he or she will probably not be able to get a loan to buy a more reliable vehicle. He or she may even have a little money on hand that he or she wants to transform into something that can be protected in bankruptcy.

There are several potential traps in bankruptcy for this type of action. First, if the money is used to outright pay for all or a great deal of the vehicle, you are back in the trap covered in the previous section. The second trap is that often the exemptions will not be available if you filed too close to when you purchased the vehicle. The seller may claim fraud if the purchase and the filing come too close together. Always check with a lawyer before you take this step. If you are in the process of filling out the paperwork for a bankruptcy, be doubly sure to talk to your bankruptcy lawyer about this. It is amazing how many people will buy cars while in the process of having the bankruptcy papers drawn up and never think to talk to a lawyer.

Hiding Assets

The most dangerous course of action when bankruptcy is near or is being filed is to hide assets. This can range from giving gold pins to a family member to hold to not listing land owned in another state or county. As with taxes, this type of fraud is hard to discover, so the government has made the punishment very harsh when it does find fraud. Often people who do this type of thing are sent to jail.

How does the government find out about it? Ex-spouses, ex-friends, and coworkers. It is amazing how much secretaries know. Creditors have lists of all the things you said you owned when you were trying to get your loan, and they do not look kindly on you trying to stiff them by hiding these assets in bankruptcy.

CHAPTER 7 BANKRUPTCY

14

Under the new law, there are a number of new issues in filing a Chapter 7 bankruptcy. Under the old law, there were few restraints to filing a Chapter 7. Now, to file a Chapter 7, a person or couple must prove that meaningful repaying of debts is not possible. This is done by passing a *means test*. The test looks at the average income from all sources for the last six months. If both spouses file for bankruptcy, both spouses' incomes are counted. If only one spouse files, though, the other spouse's income will still be counted, subject to some setoffs.

What is income and what is setoff is subject to complex, changing rules that can vary from one part of the country to another. These new rules are so complex that they have caused many lawyers to stop doing bankruptcy work.

The means test is worked out on a form titled *Statement of Current Monthly Income and Means Test Calculation*, which must be filled out. This form will help determine what can be paid to creditors based on income and setoffs.

The means test is a bit more complicated for a person who operates his or her own business. His or her income is income after business expenses. Having good business records becomes even more important than under past bankruptcy laws.

Several other steps are also required by the changed law. A *Certificate of Credit Counseling* must be filed. The credit counseling must be done before you file. After you file, you must take another financial counseling class and file a *Certificate of Financial Management Course*.

Also, almost everyone who owes money on a vehicle when they file for bankruptcy must sign and file a *Reaffirmation Agreement* for each vehicle debt. In most cases, these must be reviewed and approved by the court. Having to sign and file a Reaffirmation Agreement creates a problem. To file a Chapter 7 bankruptcy, one must show via the means test that he or she has very little money leftover. However, in order to keep his or her car, he or she must show that he or she has enough money leftover to pay for the car. Often, this leaves the person very little room to maneuver.

As in filing your taxes, the great bulk of the work in a Chapter 7 is in collecting and classifying the information. Once the information is collected, it is recorded in the petition's ten schedules, the *Statement of Financial Affairs*, and the *Statement of Intention*.

The schedules are:

Schedule A	Real property
Schedule B	Personal property
Schedule C	Property claimed as exempt
Schedule D	Creditors holding secured claims
Schedule E	Creditors holding unsecured priority claims
Schedule F	Creditors holding unsecured nonpriority claims
Schedule G	Executory contracts and unexpired leases
Schedule H	Codebtors

Schedule I   Current income

Schedule J   Current expenditures

The Automatic Stay

One of the main reasons many people file bankruptcy is to stop phone calls from creditors. The automatic stay is what accomplishes this.

The *automatic stay* is a court order forbidding contact with the debtor/petitioner by the creditor. The creditors are ordered to stop collection phone calls, letters, and lawsuits. Because of the potential damages that could be awarded against them in a legal action if they defy this court order, most creditors stop all contacts with the debtor. This can be a problem for people who plan to keep on paying a given debt and depend on the creditor sending them a bill or reminder each month. Normally, even these will stop and often people get into trouble with the creditor for not making monthly payments on items they wish to keep.

If a creditor wants to continue to try to foreclose on your home, he or she must go to court and ask the judge to lift the stay. This is often granted in a Chapter 7 case. In a Chapter 13 case, it is much harder for a creditor to have the automatic stay lifted.

Trustee

Once your petition is filed, it is given to a trustee for your case. The trustee's job is to represent the creditors in general and obtain as much money as he or she can from you. Your lawyer will use the exemptions your state provides to protect as much of your property and assets as possible.

Most of the trustee's review of your case is done in the trustee's office. In the typical case, your only contact with the trustee will be at the *Section 341 meeting*, which takes place about a month after you file. There the trustee will ask you a short series of questions with two purposes in mind. The first is designed to get you to state under oath that you put a proper value on all listed property, that you listed all your property, and that you have not improperly transferred money or property to a third person. The second purpose is to ask questions about how you came up with the listed value for your home, car, and other property.

Section 341 Meeting

The Section 341 meeting is often called a meeting of creditors or a first meeting of creditors, as this is the creditor's chance to ask questions. The ringmaster of the meeting of creditors is the bankruptcy trustee. He or she is picked, normally on a rotating basis, from a panel of trustees for the court district. The trustees are normally experienced bankruptcy lawyers. They are not paid much for handling the case and normally they are undertaking to handle a great many routine, low-paying cases for the opportunity to work on a case that has enough assets to generate fees for the trustee. The trustee is liable for oversight to be sure he or she does a complete and timely job.

Reviewing the Petition

Before you are questioned at the meeting of creditors, the trustee's office will have reviewed your petition to be sure that a fair value has been placed on listed assets, on assets that have a value in excess of the protected zone provided in their state, and on recent financial dealings. The latter include payments to creditors—especially family members—just before the filing of the Chapter 7 petition, and the giving or selling of property close to the filing. If a trustee finds you have improperly transferred property to a creditor or family member, he or she can force the recipient to return the property.

Two situations often develop. A parent has title, often for insurance purposes, for a car that is really the child's. The parent transfers the title to the child just before filing to get the legal car title in alignment with the true facts. Another common situation is that a person has borrowed money from a parent and each month makes a payment toward repaying the loan. In both of these cases, the trustee can force the recipient of the property or the money to *disgorge* (give up) what he or she has received. The value received is used to pay a fee to the trustee and is divided among other creditors.

The trustee does not normally get involved with property you choose to surrender to a creditor. He or she will merely tell you or your lawyer to make arrangements with the creditor to deliver the property or make it available for pickup if you have not already done so.

Creditor Attendance

Normally, most creditors will not bother to come and ask questions. However, sometimes creditors do attend and have questions. They may ask about statements regrading assets and income you made on a loan application. This can be very embarrassing and troublesome if the statements on the loan application are different from what is listed in your bankruptcy petition. One occasionally sees creditors call attention to business equipment or other assets not listed on the bankruptcy petition.

The questions asked by the trustee and creditors are normally low-key. Real life does not mimic television in terms of cross-examination on lawyer-based television dramas. To start with, the format of doing many cases in a short period of time does not allow lengthy questions. Second, there is normally not much need for extended questioning, as the information on the petition is accurate and complete. And the careful loan applicant will have put a fair value on all property listed in the loan application.

The atmosphere is much more casual than at a trial. There is no judge present. Normally, the trustee, the petitioner, and his or her lawyer sit fairly close to each other. There are usually not too many extra court officials at a Section 341 meeting.

Others at the Meeting

People always ask if there will be other people at the meeting, as they fear having their personal affairs put on public display. There will be other people at the meeting, but almost all of them will be other people who have filed bankruptcy, lawyers, and a few representatives of creditors. We have never seen members of the general public at a meeting of creditors the way you sometimes see at a state court trial. The meetings of creditors are too boring and out of the way to attract bystanders.

After the 341 Meeting

In the vast majority of Chapter 7 cases, the hearing marks the last step in the process that involves the petitioner. The petitioner then waits about three to five months to receive his or her discharge letter.

There may be some ministerial steps. The filer may elect to reaffirm some debts. The normal reason to do this is to keep property—such as cars—on which the creditor has a lien and could take. You should get the advice of your lawyer before signing a reaffirmation agreement.

Following the meeting of creditors, there is a short period of suspense while you wait to see if any of your creditors will challenge you or otherwise cause problems. Your creditors have sixty days from the date of the first scheduled meeting of creditors in which to challenge the discharge of their debt. The sixty-day date is called the *bar date*, as it bars creditors from raising objections after that date.

If nothing untoward happens, you should receive your discharge papers about three to five months after you file your petition. (The difference in time will depend on how fast the court system can complete its paperwork.) This letter normally states that you have received a bankruptcy discharge. It does not state which debts are discharged. For this reason, it is important to hold on to both your copy of the bankruptcy petition—which lists your creditors—and the discharge letter. They are the two halves of the whole. One shows which debts were listed and the other says that the listed debts are discharged.

Problems That Can Arise

In the great majority of cases, the meeting of creditors goes smoothly and all the petitioner needs to do is wait for his or her discharge papers. But sometimes problems do occur.

Transfers to Family

One issue has already been mentioned—transfers to family members within two years prior to the petition being filed. Another is large payments to one creditor within a short time of filing the petition. The system does not want one creditor to be favored over another. For example, if you made a $1,000 payment to one credit card company but paid nothing to the others, the trustee may make that credit card company disgorge the money.

Tax Refund

Depending on when the petition is filed, the petitioner may be entitled to or receive a tax refund within six months of the filing of the petition. It is always a surprise to people to learn that the trustee and the creditors are entitled to this money if it cannot be protected using the exemptions available in the applicable state.

Inheritances

Inheritances are another possible problem. If people are surprised to learn that the trustee has a potential claim on tax refunds, they are shocked and dismayed to learn that the trustee can take inheritances that accrue within six months of filing. In addition to the loss of a loved one, the person is faced with the loss of property that the family member spent a lifetime acquiring. This is a disaster, as the protecting exemptions allowed by state and federal law typically do not come close to protecting what has been inherited. If an inheritance occurs, the trustee will take enough of the petitioner's share of the estate to pay all filed claims and pay for his or her time. Occasionally the inherited money is sufficiently large to allow for a return of some of the money to the filer after all filed claims and administrative expenses have been paid, but this does not happen often.

Logically, the petitioner is not much worse off than he or she would have been if he or she had inherited the money the week before filing the bankruptcy petition. In such a case, he or she would have paid off the debts and kept what was left. And he or she may be better off, for often his or her share of the inheritance is not large enough to pay off the debts. But people often do not see it this way. They tend to mentally divide the money into different pots. This pot is the debt and it has to get along on its own. The other pot is the family inheritance, and it is viewed as a one-time, personal thing. Often people think about the improvements they could make to their homes, education payments they could make for their children, or dream vacations they could take. Thus, it is very painful to lose the money that would have paid for these things.

Forgetting to List Something

Sometimes in the stress and rush of preparing the bankruptcy petition, a person will find that he or she inadvertently forgot to list a debt or an asset. This can easily be overcome if it is discovered shortly after filing the petition by filing an *amendment to the petition*. If the oversight is discovered later, it can be a larger problem. The trustee or a creditor may conclude you were trying to hide the asset. And if the case has been closed without a creditor being listed, you may not have that debt discharged. Normally, only creditors listed in the bankruptcy have their debts done away with. Even in such a case there may be ways around this, but it is far better and safer to be very thorough when you supply information for the court in the original filing.

Other Problems

Other problems can come up from strict policies of creditors. Sometimes hospitals will refuse to release medical information because their debt was discharged in a bankruptcy. Other times creditors, or someone who purchased the debt, will try to collect on a debt that was listed and discharged in bankruptcy. Lenders may refuse to grant a loan until you prove that a given debt was discharged in your bankruptcy. (This often occurs because the credit report is not complete or correct.) Most of these problems can be overcome by being careful to hold on to your discharge letter and petition.

CHAPTER 11 BANKRUPTCY AND CHAPTER 13 BANKRUPTCY

15

This section will examine how Chapters 11 and 13 bankruptcies proceed. They are different from Chapter 7 bankruptcy as discussed in the previous section.

Chapter 11 Bankruptcy

The goal of a Chapter 11 bankruptcy filing is to stop the business's destructive spiral. It gives everyone time to collect the facts to see if the company, perhaps on a greatly stripped-down level, can continue to operate, or whether it should be *liquidated* (all assets sold) in an orderly manner.

In a business, the concern often has a great deal more value than the sum of its assets. Often business equipment brings in very little money when sold. This is because the assets of most businesses are so specialized that they cannot be used for other purposes by other businesses. In addition, of course, the good will and trade name are lost if the business is shut down. Society and the stakeholders in the business—employees, customers, creditors, and owners—will achieve the best value if the business can be kept alive.

Sometimes a Chapter 11 is used to avoid unwise contracts that have become an unbearable drag on the company's chance for profitability. This may be a vendor contract or a lease.

In other cases, there is a desire to sell the business assets or operation as an ongoing business. The Chapter 11 can give you time to dispose of the business in an orderly way. The filing prevents one or two creditors from destroying the business by seizing key property or assets.

Legal Steps

There are several distinct legal steps in a Chapter 11 proceeding. First, just like any other bankruptcy, a petition must be filed. This brings the individual or corporation under the protection of the bankruptcy system. Normally the owners or management will want to continue to run the business as *debtor possession*. The court has the final say over whether or not this will be allowed, but normally the interests of everyone are served by having the people who best know the business continue to operate it.

However, because the business and its property have come under the jurisdiction of the court, reports are typically required to give a running account of what is being done by the debtor in possession and in particular how assets are being disposed of. This often means filing a monthly report with the court, which can be a hard burden on an overworked small business owner. A large company could simply have an accountant create a monthly report, with court approval. A struggling small business may not be able to afford to have a third party create this report every month.

Committee of Creditors

The creditors cannot be disregarded after filing Chapter 11. The U.S. Bankruptcy Code provides for the creation of one or more *committees of creditors*. These are small groups that represent the creditors in general. This small group is often a big help to businesses that have thousands of creditors to deal with, but may not be much help to a small business that has only a few creditors to begin with.

There is a *meeting of creditors* where the debtor has the opportunity to explain his or her situation to creditors—what went wrong, and how the future of the business can be protected. The creditors have the chance to ask questions of the petitioner or his or her representative.

Independent Reports

Often an independent party is appointed to study the business and give an independent report on its problems and prospects. The petitioner is typically expected to pay the fees of this independent party.

Disclosure Statement

A *disclosure statement* must be prepared, and after approval by the court, it will be sent to creditors as part of the next legal step—solicitations for acceptance of the plan of reorganization. The disclosure statement gives a summary of the plan of reorganization and how the different types of creditors will be treated. A general overview of the finances of the filing entity is given along with what would happen if other alternatives, such as complete liquidation, were followed.

The statement also alerts the reader to risk factors involved in the different alternatives facing the business or person. A hearing on the disclosure statement is held before the statement and the plan of reorganization can be sent to interested parties. Since the disclosure statement summarizes the plan of reorganization, the plan of reorganization must be thought out early in the process.

Plan of Reorganization

The heart of the Chapter 11 is the *plan of reorganization*. It spells out how each class of creditor is to be treated. A class is one or more creditors who share similar situations. Part of the art of doing a Chapter 11 is knowing how the different creditors can be put in one or more classes as the needs of the situation require.

How creditors are classed is very important, as a vote of creditors on the plan will be taken and the approval of different classes must be obtained.

The ideal is the approval of every class that is *impaired*, or is receiving less than what is owed them. This of course may not happen, and in that case the court can *cram down* their interest (make them take less if some technical rules are followed). Since a vote of a majority of the members of a given class is required for approval by that class, the makeup of the different classes is very important.

It is a mistake to blindly put together a plan for reorganization and put it to a vote without having a pretty good idea of how key classes will vote. This way if you see a group of creditors that does not like a provision, you have the chance to change your proposal before it is written up and mailed out.

Normally, in addition to asking what the creditors think, the debtor and his or her lawyer will negotiate with the creditors about the treatment of their class. Often the creditor must be educated as to what the alternatives are. No creditor likes receiving less than what was contracted for, so the creditor must be made to see that accepting the proposal with its economic loss is better than any of the alternatives.

Often this disintegrates into a game where the creditor has the option to try to kill the reorganization by voting against the plan. The creditor uses this power to try to force better terms. The debtor wants the business to keep on operating, which is why he or she filed a Chapter 11. But the plan must leave the debtor a reasonable chance to succeed. Agreeing to an unrealistic plan provision that will surely kill the business does not help anyone at all.

Chapter 13 Bankruptcy

A Chapter 13 bankruptcy is a hybrid between a Chapter 7 and a Chapter 11. The typical Chapter 13 filer has one or more of three motivations. An important reason for many people is that the creditors will receive back some of the money they loaned you. "I made these debts and I have always paid my debts," is a common statement. People are willing to put up with the problems inherent in the Chapter 13 process because of the desire to pay at least some of their debts back.

Another reason people file Chapter 13 is to save their homes or cars. Unlike Chapter 7, a Chapter 13 is designed to stop foreclosures and repossessions. The creditor can object if the proposed Chapter 13 repayment plan is unrealistic or if the property will depreciate faster than the creditor is paid under the plan. However, given a reasonable plan, a Chapter 13 program will allow a debtor the chance to save his or her home and car and make up missed payments a little each month.

This latter factor is very important in dealing with homes. Many Chapter 13 filers are people who, for one reason or another, missed monthly house payments. Often the creditor's response is to demand that all back payments be made as a lump sum and refuse to take offered monthly payments. If a person cannot pay all back payments at once, his or her only option may be to file a Chapter 13. The other options—refinancing his or her home and debt consolidation loans—typically are not available because of the black mark on his or her credit caused by the missed house payments.

A third reason people file Chapter 13 is because it affords them the chance to retain property they would lose in a Chapter 7. Chapter 7 filers have the possibility of losing property, especially business property, no matter which state they live in. This is a problem for business owners, as state exemptions tend to concentrate on protecting people's homes and personal household-related items as opposed to protecting business property.

Much of this personal and business property can be protected in Chapter 13. As long as creditors receive at least what they would have received in Chapter 7, the Chapter 13 will work. The amount the creditors receive does not need to be paid all at once as would be the case in Chapter 7. The payment can be stretched out over the three- to five-year life of the Chapter 13.

Operation of a Chapter 13

A form very much like the means test must be filled out as part of filing Chapter 13. It is used to work out the size and term (three to five years) of the plan. Its long name is *Statement of Current Monthly Income and Calculation of Commitment Period and Disposable Income.* It looks at the average income from all sources for the last six months. Both spouses' incomes are counted if both are filing. If only one spouse files, both spouses' incomes are still counted, subject to specific setoffs for the non-filing spouse.

What is income and what is setoff is subject to complex, changing rules that can vary from one part of the country to another. The calculations are more complex for most people who operate their own business, as business expenses must be calculated alone first and set aside.

The debtor must also receive credit counseling before the filing as a *Certificate of Credit Counseling* must be filed with the petition.

The structure of a Chapter 13 petition is similar to a Chapter 7 petition. It has ten schedules, and it has a proposed plan that sets out how debts are to be paid. There is also a statement of financial affairs.

The schedules are:

Schedule A	Real property
Schedule B	Personal property
Schedule C	Property classified as exempt
Schedule D	Secured creditors

Schedule E   Priority creditors

Schedule F   Unsecured creditors

Schedule G   Executory contracts and unexpired leases

Schedule H   Codebtors

Schedule I   Current income

Schedule J   Current expenses

Proposed Plan

The heart of the Chapter 13 is the plan, which sets out how each class of creditors will be paid. It is similar to a Chapter 11 plan, but it is less complex since it is dealing with a wage earning individual or an individual who operates a small business rather than a large, complex business.

The plan will set out how long the plan will last—three to five years—and what will be paid to the trustee and to the lawyer who represented the debtor.

It will also list how the different main classes of creditors will be paid. Secured creditors may either be paid in full or partially paid in full and partially paid as unsecured creditors. Debtors may choose to pay cosigned claims in full to protect the cosigners.

The plan will state how back taxes and student loans will be treated. It will set out how fast arrearages will be repaid. The plan will also state in a general way how the *unsecured claims*—credit cards, personal loans, medical bills, etc.—will be treated. This is the *plug number* in most plans, as there is often a general understanding in a given area about what percentage must be paid to unsecured general creditors. If the proposed plan is too aggressive in limiting what is paid to creditors, the creditors can object and a court hearing will be held.

Two overarching constraints limit the plan. First, the unsecured creditors must receive at least what they would have received in a Chapter 7 bankruptcy. Second, the debtor must devote all or substantially all of his or her *disposable income* to the repayment plan. *Disposable income* is money available from income after reasonable living expenses. This opens another avenue for disputes, as a creditor or trustee may have an objection stating that a given debtor's living expenses are not reasonable.

Areas of dispute—in addition to the normal cost of food and entertainment—are expenses for charitable giving, repayment of loans against retirement plans, and the cost of private schooling for the debtor's children. The plan will also state which creditors are to be paid directly, what property is to be surrendered, and what executory contracts and leases will be kept or given up.

After the Plan is Filed

After the plan is filed, a first meeting of creditors is held where creditors can question the debtor, and then there is time allowed for the creditors to object to the plan. At the time of filing, the creditors are notified to file their claims with the court stating how much they believe they are owed. It is not uncommon for this amount to be different from what the debtor claims he or she owes. The debtor can object to the claim if he or she thinks it is incorrect. A hearing would then be held to see which party is correct.

If there are no objections by either party, the plan goes into effect as written and is binding on all parties.

Post-Plan Problems

A Chapter 13 plan lasts for three to five years, and during that time, the debtor has a special relationship with the court. In a Chapter 7 filing, the trustee takes what property he or she can and sells it. In a Chapter 13, the debtor is allowed to keep and use the property but is accountable to the court for its use. He or she is treated as a *debtor in possession of bankruptcy property* or *debtor in possession*. Since the court could have taken the property to settle debt but did not, the debtor must stand ready to account for this property.

Sale of property. The main time this debtor-in-possession theory causes a problem is when people want to sell their home or their vehicles. Since it is the property of the bankruptcy estate, people are not free to just sell the property and pocket the money. They must first obtain permission of the court for the sale and account for the money received. By the same token, you cannot, for example, just give a vehicle to your child because everyone in the family knows it is really the child's car.

New debt. While you are under Chapter 13, you are not allowed to incur more debt. This means you must stop charging on credit cards and cannot borrow money during the life of the plan without the court's or trustee's specific permission. This often causes problems when cars wear out or when the debtor must move.

Before the court will allow new or additional debt, it will want to know the terms of the new debt, what is being bought, and why. Be sure the additional debt can be repaid without hurting the old creditors.

Car wrecks. A problem that is fairly common during the life of the Chapter 13 plan is a car wreck. Sometimes it seems that car wrecks seek out people in Chapter 13. In a certain number of these wrecks the debtor's car will be totaled. This means the debtor must replace the car and will need new financing. The system allows for this financing to be done by the old lienholder, if there is one, with the old lienholder obtaining a lien on the new car.

In practice this can be a problem. If a car is totaled, the insurance company often does not pay enough to replace the car. The creditor, if it is to substitute collateral, will want a car at least as valuable as the one that was wrecked and does not care that the insurance payoff was not enough to purchase such a car. Often the creditor will refuse to allow any substitution on collateral and the debtor must ask for help from the court. All of this takes time, and the debtor may very well have to pay extra money to obtain the replacement car. This is very hard on debtors who are without a car to drive to work and short of ready cash.

Insurance lapses. When a person takes out a loan on a car, a standard clause in his or her loan agreement requires him or her to keep *collision insurance*. This will allow the lender to recover some of the loaned money if something happens to the car.

Once in a Chapter 13, people often have a hard time making ends meet. They may have suffered a drop in income or have agreed to a repayment plan they really could not quite afford in an effort to save a home or a car. To make ends meet, there is a temptation to let insurance premium payments slide.

This is a mistake. The creditor has the ability to repossess cars when the debtor fails to keep insurance on them, as required by the security agreement. The idea behind this is that the creditor is being kept by the bankruptcy filing from taking the car, and in exchange the debtor has a duty to give the creditor the protection offered by the collision insurance policy.

Drop in income. When considering filing a Chapter 13, people usually want to know what will happen if their income drops or they have unexpected expenses. This is a real problem for self-employed business owners, as their month-to-month income is not steady. They often have slower sales during certain seasons.

The short answer is that you are expected to make the Chapter 13 monthly payment whether or not you have a shortfall in a given month. Sometimes the trustee will give you a chance to make a short payment. However, this is often not much help. You will usually be expected to make increased payments until the shortfall is made up in a short period of time. Often people find themselves in a downward spiral. They could not afford to make their regular payments, and now they have to come up with the money to make their regular payments and the money to make up a missed payment. Unless the shortfall was a one-time blip, this may be impossible, and they will be dropped from the Chapter 13 program.

Post-Filing Issues

16

With a few exceptions, the filing of bankruptcy sets your financial picture. It is like a financial snapshot was taken on the day you filed your bankruptcy petition. What you have in your possession is reachable by the bankruptcy trustee, and to protect it you must use the exemptions allowed by applicable state and federal law. However, there are exceptions to this general rule.

Inheritances

In a Chapter 7 proceeding, money you inherit within six months after you file your petition is subject to being taken by the trustee for the benefit of creditors. This is always a terrible shock to people. In addition to the sadness of the loss of a loved one—usually a parent—the filer stands to lose much of what his or her family member worked so hard to build up. The general rules of exemptions apply to inheritances, but usually inheritances are so large that the exemption protection does not help much.

In a Chapter 13 proceeding, having an inheritance creates two problems. The first is because of the general rule that creditors in a Chapter 13 case should receive at least what creditors in a Chapter 7 case would have received. The second is because of the *disposable income test*. People in a Chapter 13 proceeding are supposed to devote all of their disposable income to the Chapter 13 plan. If you inherit money, you have more to pay your creditors with.

Tax Refunds

The same general rules apply to tax refunds above your protected limit. Here the *wild card*—exemptions in any asset allowed if you do not use your homestead exemption—may be useful. A $2,000 protection zone may not be very helpful in the case of an inheritance, but could be enough to protect a major portion of a tax refund. In a multiyear Chapter 13 plan, tax refunds do not normally come into consideration.

Gifts from Family or Friends

Money you receive as a gift from your family after filing a bankruptcy is normally protected. This means that a family member or a friend could purchase a car or other item for you. In many cases, such people buy items and property from the trustee as part of the sale of assets procedure and then gift them back to you.

This is particularly helpful to business owners who want to keep their business going but who need to purchase assets of the business to achieve this goal.

Deceiving the Trustee

The trustee learning about your inheritance or tax refund depends to a great extent on the honor system. There is not a central repository that lists inheritances or tax refunds. The trustee may never know about the inheritance or tax refund if you do not tell him or her. This creates a strong incentive to cheat the system by never telling anyone about it.

Not revealing assets such as inheritances and tax refunds is bankruptcy fraud, and people who hide assets are subject to federal criminal prosecution. You could go to jail. Do not expect your lawyer to help you hide these assets. Lawyers are forbidden to help people commit a crime.

Income Increases

Most of the time, in a Chapter 7 bankruptcy filing, good fortune that befalls you after you file bankruptcy is good fortune that does not need to be shared. If you land a new, higher-paying job or get a raise at your present job, the increase is yours. The idea of the Chapter 7 bankruptcy is to give you a fresh start in life. If the creditors or the bankruptcy system could reach out and seize property as you are trying to rebuild your life, this purpose would be defeated.

A Chapter 13 proceeding is different. In a Chapter 7 filing, a snapshot of one's financial affairs is taken the day you file and that is basically all there is to it. But in a Chapter 13 filing, you subject yourself and your property to the review of the court for several years. This gives time for the disposable income test to affect you.

Some Chapter 13 courts, trustees, and creditors will take the position that if you are earning more money, then you have more disposable income to pay to your creditors, and they may push for you to make larger payments. Normally, though, this is not a problem. As your income rises your reasonable living expenses will also increase. The net result is that usually no more disposable income is available for creditors.

However, this concept can be a problem for small business owners. It is not unheard of for a business to start doing well after filing for Chapter 13, which means that a lot more money is being generated for the business owner than before the case was filed. If more money is coming in, the trustee, court, or creditor may invoke the disposable income rule and call for much of this extra money to go to the Chapter 13 trustee to pay off the business's debts. The increase in available funds will often come to the attention of the Chapter 13 trustee because many of the trustees review monthly business reports from people in Chapter 13 who are operating a business.

The increase in income can come to the attention of the Chapter 13 trustee in the case of a business owner or a regular wage earner in another way. It is not uncommon for a person in Chapter 13 to need to buy another car or a new house during the three to five years the Chapter 13 plan lasts. To undertake new debts to purchase a car or house requires the permission of the court or trustee. This permission will not be forthcoming unless the person can afford the new property.

To prove they can afford the new house or car, people will reveal their higher income. With this information, the court, trustee, or creditor then invokes the disposable income rule. In a few cases, people are turned down for the house or car and are required to pay more into the Chapter 13 plan because of their higher disposable income.

Post-Filing Steps and Problems in Chapter 7 Bankruptcy

17

The filing of the bankruptcy petition does not end the bankruptcy process. There are several events that regularly occur and some that might occur after the petition is filed.

A great deal of trust is placed on the person who fills out the bankruptcy petition, but the system provides for chances to test the truthfulness of the filer. One of these chances is a meeting, called the Section 341 meeting, which is discussed in Section 14.

Audits

If there are questions about the filing, the trustee can order an audit. This can take several forms. The trustee may direct an appraiser to go out to a person's home and value the contents of the home. This is sometimes done when the filer has a very expensive home and puts a very low value on the furnishings in that home. Trustees have found by experience that people with very expensive homes tend to buy expensive, high quality furniture for those homes. Trustees may also send an appraiser to value vehicles. Sometimes old cars are not worth much at all, and sometimes they are valuable collector's items.

Under the new bankruptcy code, bankruptcy cases are also randomly audited. Every two hundred and fiftieth case is picked for review. The auditors will request bank statements with explanations of large deposits and withdrawals, among other items. This process was put in place to try to ensure honesty in the system.

In a business context, an audit or review by an appraiser is common. The greater likelihood of obtaining money from a sale makes this expense worthwhile for the trustee. Audits require the support for the statements in the bankruptcy petition. The filer will be asked to produce deeds and car titles to see what type of car the filer really owns and who owns the land and the vehicle, and bank records to see how much money is really flowing through the business and is in the individual's hands.

Challenges by the Creditors

One of the main safeguards in the bankruptcy system is that creditors or government officials overseeing the case can challenge the petition and the propriety of debt discharge. An important source of challenges is changes in the filer's borrowing and spending patterns. Sometimes people go on spending sprees just before they file for bankruptcy. They go on vacation or buy a large number of personal items. Then they try to do away with these debts through bankruptcy. Creditors have the right to challenge the discharge of these debts.

In the past, if a creditor gave a business or an individual a line of credit, it was the creditor's problem if the borrower used it. The idea was that it was the creditor's responsibility to know who it was lending money to and to get security for its loans. Today the rules are a bit different. Borrowers on *standing lines of credit*—such as credit cards—are often deemed to be making a representation of their ability and intent to repay each time they draw or charge on their line of credit. If this representation is found to be false, the creditor can move to not allow the debt to be discharged. Some creditors try to this new power by challenging many charges and leaving it up to the borrower to demonstrate that his or her motives were pure when he or she borrowed the money.

The problem with this is that the final arbitrator of the borrower's intentions is a judge, and it is expensive to have a federal trial before a judge. A trial involves many filings and appearances before the court and extensive *discovery* (gathering of evidence). The creditor has deep pockets and the bankrupt is by definition without money. Some creditors use this situation to go on fishing expeditions. They threaten challenges and then offer to settle for a lesser sum. If they can threaten enough people and induce enough people to settle, the creditors can collect a lot of money.

To stop this process from being abused, the law now provides that if the creditor brings a challenge without a reasonable basis, the creditor must pay the debtor's attorney's fees. While this does not happen in every case, it happens enough that creditors are dissuaded from making challenges without any basis in fact. Creditors will also ask why the assets and their values listed on loan applications are different from what is shown on the bankruptcy petition. If a great deal of money and assets has disappeared, the creditors will want to know what happened to it.

Challenges by Third Parties

Another element that makes the system work is that third parties often call the trustee's attention to improper actions by the filer—unhappy business associates or ex-spouses are a fruitful source of negative information. Ex-employees also often know a lot and will call the trustee's attention to improper actions or assets that have not been listed. (There was even a case where a filer tried to hide assets by buying an expensive exempt asset, filing bankruptcy, and then returning the asset for a refund. The merchant, unhappy at losing the big sale, turned the filer in.)

Criminal Sanctions

If it comes out that a filer tried to lie to the trustee or to hide assets, the filer is subject to *criminal sanctions*, which can consist of fines and time in jail.

CONTNUING IN BUSINESS AFTER BANKRUPTCY | 18

Many proprietors who run into money problems and have to consider going into bankruptcy choose to give up running their own business and take a job as an employee. Others want to continue running the business and look for ways to do so after bankruptcy. Whether they will be able to do so will depend on the nature of the business.

Every business has assets that may be lost in a bankruptcy, including assets you may not at first think of, such as business names, locations, and phone numbers. If a customer is used to calling one company at a given phone number or going to a specific location, and those things are gone after the bankruptcy, the owner will face the challenge of reopening the business under a new name. As often happens, there is a period when the service or sales cannot be made, competitors may have moved in on the account, and competition will be tougher.

Keeping a Business Alive

There is a great temptation to move tools and office equipment, particularly computers and software, away from the business location. As mentioned elsewhere, it is often not clear whether the business owns a computer, particularly a portable computer, or software. This urge must be resisted. Hiding assets from the trustee, which includes moving material from one location or category to another, is bankruptcy fraud. It can easily lead to criminal prosecution and jail time. Do not expect your lawyer to help you accomplish this fraud. The lawyer has a duty to the court to make sure the system is not cheated of assets, and the lawyer could lose his or her license if he or she knowingly allows a client to commit fraud.

Besides, it is not at all necessary to run such a risk to regain the tools and equipment. Office furniture is easy to replace. Your computer software and the records contained in them have almost no value to anyone else. For this reason, the trustee is likely to abandon them or sell them back to you for a very low price. In fact, the biggest danger is that the trustee, presuming that there is no value or utility in the software, will casually abandon it or have it destroyed. You can best help yourself here by letting the trustee know that you wish to have or buy these records and software.

Business Name

Your business name has a great deal of value. If your business was incorporated, the corporate name was listed with your state's secretary of state, and that particular name is probably protected. If you wish to keep it, you should make sure the old corporation is legally dissolved. This will free up the business name. Then, you can simply incorporate a new business with the same name, or otherwise file to protect the business or trade name. Remember, the trade or corporate name is an asset of the court, and if you have a particularly good business name, the trustee may try to sell it. Some names may be so good that someone would be willing to pay the trustee to obtain the name, but this is unlikely. There is no central exchange where people looking for business names can go, so it is hard for the trustee to find a buyer.

Business Phone Number

Another important asset of the business is the phone number. Your phone number is your lifeline as it is how most of your customers get in touch with you. Nothing signals that you are gone more definitely than the message saying, "This number has been disconnected," or for the caller to reach a private residence rather than your business.

Example:

Several years ago, we moved our office from one part of town to another, far enough away that the phone company made us use a different phone number. We let all the clients we could think of know about our new phone number. Still, our business fell off. When this happens, one never knows if it is caused by seasonal adjustments or overall business climate, but by sheer chance, we learned that our old phone number had been assigned to the child of a man we used to work with.

After about a year and a half, he told us that it was still a real problem for his son. His son was getting phone calls meant for us all the time, and his answering machine was being filled with messages meant for us. This one-in-a-million set of circumstances let us see both sides of how important a phone number can be. We were wondering where our business had gone, and the boy was being aggravated by unwanted business calls.

If you want to continue your phone service, the answer is once again fairly simple. The phone number has absolutely no value to the trustee and he or she will likely sell it to you for a normal price or just allow you to have it back. You must, in addition, be sure that the monthly bill is paid to the phone company so it does not cut off service, and ensure that it records the formalities of moving ownership from the corporation to you or your new company.

Business Location

Location can also be important to your business. Many businesses want to keep operating in the same location, since that is where their customers know to find them. In addition, most businesses draw their customers from a specific geographic area. Simply put, they come to you because you are convenient. If you move to another part of town, they may find a new business to frequent.

It is possible to keep the same location, but it does involve a bit more risk and trouble. If the corporation owns the building or land, it will be very difficult to keep the same location. The building and land normally have value and a ready market into which the trustee can sell. You, on the other hand, likely do not have any money to buy them from the trustee.

Keeping your location is easier if the space is leased. The space is normally a liability to the trustee, as he or she has to keep on paying the rent if he or she is going to try to sell the lease. The market for such a sale may be narrow as most leases limit subleases and what types of business can be operated in the space. Normally, the trustee will give up his or her right to the space fairly casually.

Your landlord may be more of a problem. You very well may have stopped paying him or her for a period of time while your business was going downhill. He or she may not be interested in having you continue as a tenant and may be happy to get rid of you without having to go through the legal steps of eviction. On the other hand, it is a lot easier on him or her to have you in the space. He or she has little downtime in receiving rent, and will not have to do any upfitting. If you want to stay in the same location, by all means talk to the landlord. Often you will be surprised at what a landlord is willing to do with you if you can present a realistic case on how you can pay your rent in the future.

Creditors and Other Problems

Remember, though, that there are problems with keeping everything the same. Creditors are likely to feel that the bankruptcy was just a sham. They may continue to make collection efforts against you as the proprietor. It can be very difficult to explain to them or the court that you are not the same entity.

Another problem with continuing the business after the bankruptcy is that for a period of time the business will be closed. In a Chapter 7 bankruptcy, operations must stop and the assets are sealed. To avoid a "Going out of Business" sign, most proprietors put out a more ambiguous sign such as "Closed for Inventory," "Closed for Remodeling," or even "Closed for Vacation." While this will not fool anyone who is closely monitoring the location for very long, it may help with casual customers who come by only once every month or two, as by the time they come back, you are back in business.

Rebuilding Credit 19

People who have gone through a financial storm normally have one of two reactions—they never want to obtain credit again, or they wonder if they can ever get credit in the future.

Reasons to Have Credit

Some clients say, "I never want to see another credit card or owe anything." While understandable, this may be an overreaction and counterproductive. While one can exist just fine without a credit card, one will sooner or later need a car or will have to move and buy a new home or rent an apartment. To do any of these things will require a reasonable credit rating. If a person does nothing to rebuild his or her credit standing, he or she may not be able to qualify for the car, house, or apartment. This means that you should work on developing your credit standing by using your credit a little. This way, you will have a better credit record should you ever need it.

Obtaining Credit After Bankruptcy

There is a common misconception that people who have filed bankruptcy can never receive credit again. Rest assured—you can have credit again. There is too much potential profit for financial institutions to cut you off from credit for very long. How long will it be before institutions will extend credit, and what can be done to shorten the time?

Time

It is hard to give a firm rule on how long it will take to receive credit again. There is no law saying when you are entitled to credit again—it is up to the individual bank or business. However, there are millions of banks and creditors in the country. Some of these banks and creditors are liberal in extending credit, while others will pass up a sale or loan if you ever filed bankruptcy.

Time is one of your great allies. The more time that has passed since you declared bankruptcy, the less the bankruptcy will affect you. Most of the time, you should be well on your way back to having a normal credit rating within two to five years of declaring bankruptcy. This will be a bit faster if you work hard on rebuilding your credit. Within two to five years, you should be able to qualify for mainstream credit cards. Of course, it will probably take longer to get back an A-rating in applying for a mortgage.

Reaffirming Credit Cards

It is not easy to obtain new credit. You may wonder why you should not reaffirm some of the debts you had prior to bankruptcy if regaining access to credit takes so much time and is so difficult. All you have to do is pay off the balance you owe on the debt, and you will have a credit card you can charge on or a loan company you can go to for future loans.

Bankruptcy lawyers usually counsel against reaffirming a debt. To understand why this is a bad idea, you need to understand the *reaffirmation process*. Say you owe $2,000 on a credit card. You sign an agreement in your bankruptcy petition that you promise to pay the debt in spite of having the right to get rid of it entirely as part of the bankruptcy process. The implied trade-off for reaffirming your debt is that you will be allowed to keep the card and use it in the future. However, some credit cards issuers revoke your credit card once you file bankruptcy. Once the card is revoked, you do not get it back just by reaffirming the debt. Instead, all you have done is taken on a debt that you did not have to pay, without receiving any benefit for doing so.

If you get lucky, and the bank does not revoke your credit card, it will almost certainly lower your credit to the amount you owe. Thus, if you owe $2,000, then your credit limit will be lowered to $2,000. In effect, you cannot use the card to charge anything until you pay off part of the $2,000 you owe. And remember, making the minimum payments each month will not make the starting balance go down much at all. You will need to make monthly payments that are a lot larger than the minimum payment to be able to use the card.

Meanwhile, do not forget you are starting out at your credit limit. It is very easy to use the card anyway and end up having an overcharge applied against your account. These charges are becoming larger as lenders search for more ways to make money. The fact that you are at your limit because you reaffirmed the debt and had your limit lowered will not make one bit of difference.

The most important reason to think long and hard about reaffirming a credit card debt is that you, in all likelihood, will not be able to pay down the debt fast enough to use the card. Most people who file Chapter 7 bankruptcy do not have any money left over from their paycheck after their living expenses are deducted. In fact, most have living expenses higher than their monthly income. The factor that is allowing them to survive month to month is that insurance and taxes do not have to be paid each month and clothes are bought irregularly.

Taking on another bill may be the straw that breaks your back. If you run into repayment problems on the reaffirmed debt, then you are in real trouble. Having a bad payment history after declaring bankruptcy is worse than having a bad payment history prior to declaring bankruptcy. It shows that you have not learned your lesson.

However, if you do have extra funds left over after paying your living expenses, you can probably afford to pay down a credit card, and if you have a real need for credit, then think about reaffirming a debt or two. Choose which credit card to reaffirm carefully. It is far better to reaffirm a credit card with a $500 limit than one with a $2,000 limit. Your goal is to have a credit card or two to use and rebuild your credit, not to be able to brag about how much credit you have available.

Next, be sure the credit card you keep is one that reports to the credit bureaus. Some department store credit cards do not report to the credit bureaus. Pick a major credit card, which will be reported. Having a major credit card can help you get the right department store and gas company credit cards when the proper time comes.

Scorekeeping

If you are serious about rebuilding your credit in the fastest possible time, you need to learn how your credit rating is determined.

Much of the credit rating in this country is done by a California company named the *Fair Isaac Corporation (FICO)*. It licenses its program to determine credit-worthiness to the three big credit bureaus and other businesses that may want to determine whether or not to make loans to someone.

Fair Isaac was one of the first and best companies to use complex mathematical algorithms, crunched on computers to predict borrowers' future actions. Developing consumer financial profiles produces a large part of the company's $270–$280 million revenue. To protect this income stream, it has tried hard to keep the factors that are considered in its algorithms and how they are multiplied a secret. For this reason, anyone writing on credit rebuilding prior to June 2000 relied purely on intuition, observation, and guesswork.

Fair Isaac scores are used by about 75% of the country's mortgage lenders and all three major credit bureaus. Each bureau has its own name for the score, but they are all based on the Fair Isaac score. These scores have been used for decades in consumer loans and credit cards under a heavy veil of secrecy. But, controversy developed as the score method moved into the mortgage industry. All aspects of people's lives were being controlled by a small group in California without accountability and in total secrecy.

The reason Fair Isaac gave for its secrecy was that the public needed more than just their scores to understand their credit standing and how to improve it—they needed additional information and individual counsel from a lender. Of course, this ignored the fact that no lender was giving any additional information to the consumer to tell him or her how to improve his or her score.

In fact, Fair Isaac's entire business depends on this information not coming out. If consumers know exactly how the scores work, they can change their actions and standing and undercut the predictive value of the product the company is selling. Likewise, if the information gets out, competitors can gain insight into the formulas and factors that the company is selling.

This raw display of power created a disturbance, and at last state governments and the Federal Trade Commission (FTC) got involved. The California Senate began to consider whether to pass a law to make Fair Isaac reveal all. In July 1999, Fair Isaac made a presentation of some of the factors used in determining a consumer's credit score. It gave examples of twelve factors and how differences in them would give different points. The higher the score, the more creditworthy one is.

12 Examples of Factors that Determine a Person's FICO Score

Own/Rent	Own	Rent	Other	No Info				
	25	15	10	17				
Years at Address	<0.5	0.5–2.49	2.5–6.49	6.5–10.49	10.49+	No Info		
	12	10	15	19	23	13		
Occupation	Professional	Semi-Professional	Manager	Office	Blue Collar	Retired	Other	No Info
	50	44	31	29	25	31	22	27
Years on Job	<0.5	0.5–1.49	1.5–2.49	2.5–5.49	5.5–12.49	12.5+	Retired	No Info
	2	8	19	25	30	39	43	20
Department Store/Major Credit Cards	None	Department Store	Major Credit Card	Both	No Answer	No Info		
	0	11	16	27	10	12		
Bank Reference	Checking	Savings	Both	Other	No Info			
	5	10	20	11	9			
Debt Ratios	<15	15–25	26–35	36–49	50+	No Info		
	22	15	12	5	0	13		
Number Inquiries	0	1	2	3	4	5–9	No Info	
	3	11	3	-7	-7	-20	0	
Years in File	<0.5	1–2	3–4	5–7	8+			
	0	5	15	30	40			
Number of Revolving Trades	0	1–2	3–5	6+				
	5	12	8	-4				
% Balances Available	0–15%	16–30%	31–40%	41–50%	50% +			
	15	5	-3	-10	-18			
Worst Credit Derogatory Description	No Record	Any Derogatory Description	Any Slow	1 Satisfactory Line	2 Satisfactory Lines	3 Satisfactory Lines		
	0	29	-14	17	24	29		

(The first line in each block is the individual's status. The second line is the points allocated for that status.)

For more information, see the FTC website at **www.ftc.gov**. Clearly, these twelve factors are not all the factors. Fair Isaac once stated that even a simple credit scoring system is likely to have 10,000–20,000 different possible combinations. The total scores range from 300 to 900 points. This means that the few elements given in the government briefing cover only a part of this possible score range.

Fair Isaac claims that it only uses financial information in its credit scoring formula. Factors such as the part of town one lives in, race, sex, and nationality are not considered. Some people doubt this claim—Fair Isaac once said age was not considered, but the data it presented at the briefing uses years in the credit file as a proxy, and one of its slides lists age as a factor in evaluating the credit applicant.

As you look at the sample chart, you will see that there are many factors you cannot affect in your efforts to rebuild your credit standing. But there are several things you can do.

- Stay at one address and do not move around a lot.

- When you do obtain credit, make timely payments.

- Do not switch jobs too often.

- If you are running your own business, especially if it is a new business, you may wish to consider taking a part-time job so your report shows employment with the steady income.

You can obtain a copy of your FICO score by using the Internet. This can be obtained through a website maintained by Fair Isaac, as well as one maintained by Equifax. The Fair Isaac site is **www.myfico.com**.

Rebuilding Your Credit

There are a number of steps you can take to rebuild your credit. Read this section closely for the best ones you should take first.

Make Sure You Have Clean Credit Reports

While you are working on rebuilding your credit, you will need to keep an eye on your credit report. The FICO score uses information in your credit report, so you will want to make sure it is up-to-date and accurate. Be sure to order a credit report from each of the three major credit reporting agencies because the information on each of them can be different and you never know which one a potential credit extender will use. The three major credit unions are:

Equifax
800-685-1111
www.equifax.com

Experian
888-397-3742
www.experian.com

TransUnion
877-332-8228
www.transunion.com

Everyone is entitled to one free credit report from each of the three agencies once a year. You can get your free credit reports by going to:

www.annualcreditreport.com

If you do not want to order your credit report online, this website provides the addresses you need to write to in order to have your free credit reports mailed to you. You will be able to get your credit report, but if you want to receive your FICO score, it will cost you extra (usually under $10 from each agency.)

Once you have your credit reports, go over hard copies of them carefully, as it is possible for them to contain mistakes. The credit bureaus are private companies that for the most part rely on what other private companies tell them. You might find that there is data for another person in your file, or that it does not show debt as being paid off or discharged in bankruptcy.

Fix errors. If there is an error, be sure to file a claim with the credit agency to correct it, either through its online dispute form or via mail. If you have received a discharge of certain debts in bankruptcy, send the credit union a copy of your bankruptcy discharge letter and a list of debts that were discharged. Challenge debts that are not yours or that are wrong. By law, the credit bureau must go back to the reporting company and ask for documentation of the entry. Ideally the company will look at its records, note the entry is wrong, and have it corrected. Often the company will not bother to respond. If it does not, the entry must be taken off your credit report.

Even though you will have to pay a nominal fee if you order more than one credit report from each agency every year, if you have recently declared bankruptcy, you should order copies of your credit report every three to six months. This will allow you to track how your credit rebuilding efforts are working.

Check Court Records

Often people who had judgments against them have paid them off, but the court records do not show this. People usually assume that once they have paid off the debt, the judgment will disappear. This is often not the case. The court system has no way of knowing if you paid off a judgment or not. For a judgment to be marked satisfied, someone, normally the judgment holder, must advise the court system that the judgment has been paid.

Many creditors simply do not bother to do this. They have their money and that is all they care about. Spending time to contact and inform the court that you have finished paying them is extra work that they do not make any money doing.

It is up to you to be sure that paid-off judgments are removed from the court records. First, check the judgment book at the courthouse where the court that entered the judgment is located. Be sure each judgment is marked "satisfied." It is very important to have judgments shown as paid because unpaid judgments are automatically picked up by the credit agencies and hurt your credit score.

If a judgment has not been marked as paid, you will need to contact the creditor and have it report to the court that the judgment was satisfied. Often, the best you can get from the creditor is a letter that says the judgment was paid. You will have to do the legwork to get this information to the court.

Work to Rebuild Your Credit

The first step is to realize that your credit rating is a statement of how likely a lender is to make money off of you. To determine this, lenders look at several factors.

- First, are other companies making money off of you? That is, do you have other debts and are you paying them regularly and on time? We cannot overemphasize the importance of making your payments on time.

- Next, do you have blemishes on your record—have you had foreclosures, repossessions, bankruptcies, and charge offs?

- Third, are you stable? Do you have ties to the community and a regular job? Lenders want to know how likely you are to skip town and how easy you will be to find.

- Fourth, do you have a regular flow of income? A nice job with a regular income is best. Worst is having no job at all. Somewhere in between is being self-employed. At best, a self-employed person or small business owner has an irregular income—up some months and years and down in others. When the income is down, it will be hard—if not impossible—to make the regular payments that creditors want.

Be careful whom you go to for credit and how you do it. There is a feeling among people who study the art of rebuilding credit that going to high-interest credit cards, subprime markets, or even finance companies will not help you much, and may even hurt you. Therefore, be careful of credit card solicitations you receive while you are in bankruptcy or just after you come out of bankruptcy. These are often high-interest, high-cost cards.

Credit for a fee. Be especially careful of letters offering to obtain a credit card for you for a fee. Often the only thing these companies are interested in obtaining is your fee. They will forward your application to several credit card companies—often high-interest ones. You could do the same thing yourself with a little research. The result of this is that you will be out the unnecessary fee you paid. Additionally, you will have a large number of credit inquiries on your credit record, which is a FICO negative, and you will probably end up only receiving offers to get high-interest cards.

As you apply for credit, be careful not to get too many credit inquiries on your record. When people want to re-establish their credit standing, a lot of them send out a large number of credit card applications, hoping that one of them will be accepted. Unfortunately, the very act of sending out the applications to several lenders lessens the chance of receiving approval.

Phones. While much of a FICO score is beyond your control, there are some things you can affect. One of the first things you should do is have a phone in your name. When people begin to have financial trouble, it is not unusual for their phone service to be cut off because they were unable to pay their phone bill each month.

In most places, a landline phone is considered a public utility, and the phone company will have to provide you with phone service. However, the phone company can minimize the risk of you not paying your bills by requiring a deposit. The amount of the deposit will vary. Whatever the phone company asks for, you should still try to get a phone. Lack of a phone shows the lack of stability, and this can hurt you as you try to rebuild your credit.

Be careful of phone services that cater to people who have had their phone service cut off. Using them will place you in a pool of people with risky credit and may work against you. Try to obtain phone service from one of the major phone companies in your area.

Bank accounts. Next, open bank checking and savings accounts. Understand that many banks will not open a new account for people who have bounced checks in the past. Some banks will not open checking accounts for people who have bad credit. This is not a universal practice, but it does happen. If you are opening a new account, talk to the bank officer and ask what the bank's policy is. While being turned down for a checking or savings account will probably not be reported to the credit bureaus, it is not worth the chance.

Secured bank loans. After you have a savings and checking account at your bank, start thinking about obtaining a secured loan from that bank. A secured bank loan is a loan that is secured by the available funds in your account. For example, if you have $500 in your savings account, you would obtain a secured bank loan of $500 or less. The bank will put a lock on your money so that if you do not pay, the bank is fully protected and will be able to take the money out of your account. While it might seem like this type of loan would be easy to obtain because the bank is protected, keep in mind how loan officers are graded. If they make a loan that goes bad, it becomes a black mark on their record and hurts their chances of promotion. This means that the loan officer is likely to be careful about making a loan to you. This is another case where you should talk with the bank officer to try to find out ahead of time if he or she will make the loan.

Remember, the bank will request data from the credit bureaus in considering the loan, and too many inquiries can hurt you. You want each inquiry made to actually result in a loan. While it is extra work to take the time to sit down and talk with the loan officer, you have had a financial mishap and will probably need to do the work if you want to speed up your credit availability.

Once you have the secured loan, make sure you pay it back on time. Your goal is to have a satisfactory line on your credit report for that loan for the FICO score-keepers to take into account. We suggest that you do not use the loan at all—put it in the bank so that you will have the money there to make each payment on time. The purpose of obtaining this loan is not so you can go out and buy a car or go on a shopping spree. Instead, the purpose of the loan is to gain a good post-bankruptcy rating on your credit report. Think of the loan interest you pay on the loan as the price you pay for the good entry.

Secured credit cards. Another source of secured loans is secured credit cards. These work in much the same way as a secured bank loan. For example, you deposit $500 into the bank that issues the secured credit card, and the bank gives you a credit limit of $500. Secured credit cards used to be hard to find, but the Internet has made finding them easier.

Before you settle on a secured credit card, ask the bank how long it will be until your credit limit is raised beyond what you have deposited in the bank if you have a perfect payment history. Some banks, no matter how well you do making your payments, will not give you unsecured credit. Your job is to find the bank that will.

You may receive offers in the mail for secured credit cards. Be very careful in accepting these offers—having a credit card from one of these companies may actually end up working against you.

Before you sign up, call the company and ask some important questions, including the following.

- Does it report to the major credit bureaus? If so, which ones?

- Does it report your card as a secured credit card? If it does, it will probably not help you rebuild your credit.

- How long is your grace period on monthly payments? Too short a grace period will cause you to pay extra interest. The worst is when interest starts accruing from the date of charge.

- Is there an application fee? If so, the lower the fee, the better.

- What is the minimum and maximum deposit required or allowed in setting up an account? A low balance can create just as successful a payment entry as a high one.

- With a good payment history, how long will it take to qualify for an unsecured credit card? Aim for twelve to eighteen months.

- How much of the deposit is available for use on the credit card? You do not want to give a security deposit of $1,000 and have a credit line of $500.

- What is the interest rate on outstanding balances? Some banks charge a very high interest rate. All other things being equal, a lower interest rate is better.

- Is there an annual service fee? Not having an annual service fee or having a very low fee is best, but it can be hard to find for a secured credit card.

- Does the company pay you interest on the security deposit you make?

- Does it deal with people in your state? Some banks will not deal with out-of-state residents and others block out certain states.

Other things to look for are a toll-free customer service number and automated customer assistance. You will want to check your credit balances often to make sure you are not going over your limit, and it is nice to be able to check twenty-four hours a day.

If you have an IRS lien or owe back taxes, some banks may not give you a secured credit card. If you have this problem, ask about the bank's policy before sending any money.

Also ask about other rules. Make sure the lender has a working phone number, street address, income requirements, and no ongoing lawsuits. Sometimes it is possible to obtain an unsecured credit card, but these often require high up-front fees, offer a low credit line, and charge high interest rates.

It takes time to process paperwork and money for a post-bankruptcy secured or unsecured credit card. If you are in a hurry, you should start early. Most banks will not issue a card until you have received your discharge papers, but you can start talking with them before you actually have the papers in your hand. Many banks will send out the application form prior to you receiving your discharge papers, with the understanding that you must wait to send the application in until you actually receive the discharge. Most banks will want a copy of your discharge papers. You can speed up the process by sending a certified check or money order rather than a personal check.

At what point in time your secured card can be turned into an unsecured one will often depend on a specific length of time. Also, your FICO score will depend in part on how long you have been making timely payments on your debts. So, it makes sense to get an early start.

Remember, your payment history only helps you if it is reported to a credit bureau—so ask the bank if it reports your payments to the credit bureaus, and then, after a few months, order a copy of your credit report to be sure they are being reported. You do not want to waste your time working with a bank that does not report to the credit bureaus.

Some banks that issue secured credit cards report to the credit bureau that the card is a secured card. It probably will not do you much good to dutifully pay on a credit card that is noted as secured in your credit file. Try hard to find a bank that does not report the fact that it is secured.

Credit Cards

You should think through why you are seeking a credit card. Is it a necessity? Having to travel and make hotel and airline reservations are often given as reasons why a person must have a credit card. Another reason is convenience. It is easier and safer to carry a credit card than a pocket full of cash. A third reason is to have a source of funds for an emergency.

Convenience. Credit cards are convenient—perhaps too convenient. It is easy to whip out the plastic when you want to buy something without really thinking about the overall, long-term cost. This is what gets most of us in trouble. For day-to-day purchases, a credit card is not really any better than carrying cash. Most purchases—such as dry cleaning, food, and gas—are for relatively small amounts of less than $100. Carrying a few twenty dollars bills in your wallet will allow you to make these purchases.

Opening your wallet psychologically makes you think about the purchase. You are more likely to elect to pass up the item, or at least remember you already spent your money, when you are considering another purchase. Credit cards are, of course, absolutely necessary for ordering items over the Internet or by phone. However, most items purchased over the Internet or from a mail order catalog are not necessities. Not buying these items is a good place to start to bring your spending under control.

Emergencies. It will be awhile before you will have the use of a credit card for a real source of funds for an emergency. If you reaffirm a credit card debt, you will start off with a low credit line or no credit line at all. If you obtain a secured credit card, the credit limit will be so low it will not be much help in a true emergency.

Building credit. For the next year or so, there is only one reason you want a credit card—to build a history of making your monthly payments in a timely way. For this reason, you will need to use your card for a few purchases and make your payments on time. If you keep a balance, it should be low. You want to have an outstanding balance of less than 15% of your available credit for a maximum score in that FICO category.

Department Store Cards

Another source of credit is department store cards. Department stores come in all sizes—from national chains to small one- or two-store operations. Often they will be more liberal in offering credit cards than the major credit card issuers. If you choose to try to obtain a department store card, be careful to investigate it beforehand. A request for credit may very well cause an inquiry on your credit report, so be sure to first try to get an idea if the store will accept you and issue a card before filling out the application. In addition, make sure it will report your timely payments to the credit bureaus. You should look into obtaining a department store credit card because having both a major credit card and a department store card gets you extra FICO points.

Car Loans

While you can control the number of credit card applications you send out, you have less control over the number of inquiries that are made. If you should try to buy a car and obtain financing, you are on dangerous ground. It is customary among car dealers to take your financial information and shop your case among many lenders. This is known as *shotgunning*. The people at Fair Isaac say their formulas take shotgunning into account and compensate for it so it does not hurt you, but there is no way to confirm that this is true.

When you are in the credit rebuilding stages and need a vehicle, you should shop for the financing before you shop for the vehicle, instead of the other way around. Once you have secured financing, then you can pick a car from what is available. While you might not be able to purchase your dream car using this method, you should still be able to get a car.

Houses

Getting on track to buy a home can take longer than qualifying for a credit card. More money is at stake so lenders are more careful. There are several different ways to purchase a home that you should consider.

Higher down payment. First, the more money you can give as a down payment, the easier, and sooner, it will be until you can qualify for a home loan. It will be almost impossible to qualify for a 5% down loan for several years, but it will be easier to qualify for a 20% down loan. Of course, this is of limited help if you have recently filed bankruptcy because you will have very little extra money for a down payment.

Another idea is to try to obtain a Federal Housing Administration (FHA) loan. The FHA will often make loans with smaller down payments.

Owner financing. *Owner financing* is another possibility, although if you have recently filed for bankruptcy, it will be harder to find an individual willing to finance your home purchase. In some cases, a seller will finance either the entire mortgage or a portion of the mortgage. Most sellers want a clean sale, but sometimes sellers who are having trouble selling their home or who for tax reasons are looking for a stream of monthly payments will consider this type of transaction. It does not hurt to ask.

Land contract or lease with option. Another possibility is a *land contract* or a *lease with an option to buy.* We suggest you stay away from this type of transaction as too many things can go wrong and cause you to lose your payments and the house. If you use this option, make sure you have your lawyer draw up the papers.

Mortgage brokers. Many people turn to *mortgage brokers* to find lenders. There are many good mortgage brokers, but just as many bad ones. Mortgage brokers are paid very well if a deal goes through, but make nothing if the loan is not made. They are highly motivated to get the job done. Unfortunately, some will put you in a subprime lending situation, often with balloon notes. Some dishonest mortgage brokers will tell you that you are getting a loan with one set of terms, but present you with a completely different set of terms at closing. In many circumstances when this happens, people feel pressured into accepting the new, less-attractive terms because without a mortgage, they will not be able to buy and move into their new home. If you use a mortgage broker to find a loan, hire your own lawyer to review the proposed loan and to attend the closing with you.

You may be told to take the loan at these terms and that after a year of good payments the terms will change. Do not depend on this happening. We see people all the time who have been told this and then cannot get the terms changed. Expect to wait at least three to six years before you can buy a house with normal financing. In the mean time, work on rebuilding your credit.

Self-employed people. Self-employed people have a harder time obtaining loans since they have irregular income, which tends to make lenders uneasy. Having a more difficult time buying a house is one of the costs of being your own boss.

If you are self-employed and really want to speed up rebuilding your credit, it is far easier to obtain a job with a steady income, even a part-time job that gives you time to also work on rebuilding your own business. This will give you a steady income, which will help you rebuild your credit faster.

Living without Credit

While rebuilding their credit, people often worry about their ability to travel. Airlines require you to buy your tickets online or over the phone, and most hotels are set up to have you guarantee your reservation with a credit card. An easy solution to this is to use a debit card to buy your airplane tickets and make reservations. Most debit cards work like a credit card, but the money comes directly out of the bank account they are linked to instead of being paid at a later time. Most hotels, if you make reservations directly through them, do not charge your card until you arrive.

If you will be traveling a lot, ask the hotel about programs they offer for frequent guests. At some hotels, after a certain amount of regular use and payments, users can guarantee reservations without a credit card or deposit. If you are using your debit card for guaranteeing room reservations, though, call the hotel and find out how much money is frozen when you make a reservation or check into a hotel. Often, the hotel locks a certain amount above the room rate in case you make long-distance calls, take something out of the mini-bar, or cause damage to the room. You do not want to overdraw your bank account because of a hotel deposit.

Conclusion

Most economists agree that the driving force of the American economy is small businesses, which in addition to creating the most new jobs are also a constant source of innovation. Some observers think that this is because Americans are natural entrepreneurs, but others point to a national system that nurtures entrepreneurship and the formation of small businesses.

A key component of this system is the bankruptcy laws and their provisions that allow individuals and businesses a fresh start. In many countries, if a business fails and the owner has many debts—particularly business debts that he or she cannot repay—the business owner will be ruined for life. With this type of economic life-or-death gamble, far fewer people are willing to take on the risks of starting their own businesses. In the United States, as this book is designed to show, when a business owner runs into financial problems, he or she does not have to deal with permanent financial failure.

Bankruptcy provides a mechanism to recover from hard times and a chance to start over. The bankruptcy system in the United States is fairly complex, and just what type of fresh start a given business owner will have varies from state to state. But no matter where you live, you are protected and afforded a chance to recover without losing everything. These are invaluable tools for the business operator.

They allow the owners to get up, dust themselves off, and go back to developing their products or business concepts and keep providing for their families.

The odds of financial problems developing during the life of a small business are high. Bankruptcy is the antidote that allows the small business owner to function and prosper for the long term in this environment. It is a tool that every small business owner should be aware of.

GLOSSARY

A

accelerate. When a debtor fails to meet a requirement of the loan—such as making timely payments—and the creditor calls for the entire loan balance to be paid at once.

accounts receivable. Money owed to a business or person that has not yet been paid.

adjustable rate mortgage (ARM). A mortgage where the interest rate can, after a set period of time, move up or down depending on the interest rate to which it is tied. These changes can happen several times over the life of the mortgage and cannot normally be halted by a bankruptcy court.

automatic stay. An order issued by the bankruptcy court stopping collection action against the person or business that filed bankruptcy.

B

bankruptcy estate. The sum of the property and assets owned by the person or business who filed bankruptcy.

bankruptcy trustee. A person appointed by the court to protect the rights of the bankruptcy filer's creditors.

bought account. A debtor's promise to pay creates an expectation of future payments. The rights to these future payments can be purchased by a third party. The third party then becomes entitled to receive payments from the debtor.

C

Chapter 7. A type of bankruptcy filed by either a corporation or an individual. It provides for the cancellation of certain unsecured debts without a repayment plan and may call for the sale of some of the filer's assets.

Chapter 11. A type of bankruptcy filed by either a corporation or an individual (but normally by a corporation). It provides for the reorganization of the filer's debts and provides for a plan of repayment of the debts in whole or part.

Chapter 12. A type of bankruptcy for family farms.

Chapter 13. A type of bankruptcy filing for individuals with regular income. It provides for the repayment, in whole or part, of the individual debts through regular payments to a Chapter 13 trustee over a period of three to five years.

civil lawsuit. A lawsuit against a person or entity that does not carry a criminal penalty. Lawsuits to collect debts by individuals or entities are almost always civil rather than criminal, and therefore a debtor is not in danger of going to jail.

collateral. Property that is promised by a borrower as security for a loan. *See* lien.

contingent debt. A debt that you may have to pay if an agreed upon event takes place.

corporate shield. Protection whereby operating as a corporation (in most cases) protects officers, directors, and shareholders from personal liability for injuries to third parties and business debts of the corporation. (This is sometimes known as the *corporate veil.*)

corporation. A type of legal entity set up under state law that is treated for many purposes as a separate person.

creditor. A person or business that has money owed to it.

credit rating. A score that rates a person's or business's creditworthiness. It is often used in deciding whether or not to make a loan to that person or business.

credit report. A report produced by a credit bureau showing a person's or business's debts and repayment history.

D

debtor. A person or business that owes money to another.

default. The failure by a debtor to act as required in a loan contract. This is normally a failure to make payments on a debt when due.

dischargeable debt. Debts that can be canceled in a bankruptcy.

discharge of debts. A bankruptcy court action or order that cancels certain debts and forbids creditors from making efforts to collect the discharged debts.

E

Employee Retirement Income Security Act (ERISA). A law enacted in the 1970s that aims to protect employee retirement funds. It sets conditions that sponsors (normally employers) must meet to claim tax benefits for contributions to a retirement or other benefit program.

equity. The value of a piece of property after deducting liens.

exempt property. Property a debtor is allowed to keep in bankruptcy.

F

foreclosure. A legal process whereby a lienholder (mortgage holder) moves to take land and any buildings on it.

freeze. In a financial transaction, it takes place when a person or entity holding funds refuses to release those funds because of a breach by the owner of the funds. For example, when a debtor fails to pay back a loan to a bank and the bank holds on to money in the debtor's savings account.

H

hardship withdrawal. The right to withdraw funds from tax-qualified pension or retirement savings when an unexpected emergency occurs or there is a pressing need for the funds.

home equity loan. A loan secured by an interest in the borrower's home. It creates a mortgage against the home.

J

judgment. An order of a court. If the order states that money is owed, it is a *money judgment.*

judgment lien. A money judgment that attaches against property. The judgment lien must be paid when the home is sold or refinanced. It is possible in some cases to remove a judgment lien in a bankruptcy.

judgment proof. A person or business that has no assets a creditor can reach to collect court-awarded judgments. In most states, a debtor may protect a certain amount of assets despite the fact that a creditor has a judgment against him or her. If the debtor's assets are within the protected limits, the creditor may not collect on the judgment.

L

lead time. A period of time in advance of an expected action or event. It is normally used to prepare for the expected action or event or to perform an action.

leasor. An individual or entity that allows the use of property in exchange for periodic payments. Most common is when a person or entity allows the use of an apartment in exchange for monthly payments.

lien. A claim by a creditor against property of the debtor to ensure that a debt is paid. Common examples of liens are loans secured by a claim against a vehicle and mortgages on homes.

M

meeting of creditors (Section 341 meeting). A bankruptcy hearing where creditors and the trustee are allowed to question a bankruptcy filer about his or her financial affairs.

money judgment. A court order directing the payment of money.

mortgage. A lien or claim against real property given to a creditor. The most common usage is a claim against one's home in exchange for the lending of money.

P

partnership. A joining together by two or more individuals to achieve a goal, such as running a business. The partnership may be formal, created by signed agreements, or informal, with no written documents. General partners are personally liable for all partnership debts.

personal guarantee. A promise by a person or business to pay a debt that is not backed by a security interest. Often it is a promise to pay a debt if another person does not pay it. It makes the person giving the guarantee fully responsible for any portion of the debt that is not paid to the lender.

petitioner. A person or corporation that has filed for bankruptcy.

piercing the corporate veil. In some cases, if corporate shareholders or officers have acted improperly or failed to follow corporate formalities, the protection offered by the corporate shield can be lifted.

plan. In bankruptcy, the written description filed by an individual or a corporation describing how debts will be treated. Bankruptcy plans are used in Chapter 11 and Chapter 13 bankruptcy filings.

process server. One who delivers lawsuit papers. Can be law enforcement personnel or an authorized private individual 18 years old or older. The term normally refers to a private individual.

property. An item that has value. It can be land, accounts receivable, investments, household or business goods, vehicles, land, etc.

proprietor. A person who owns or operates a business.

prorate. A method of sharing funds among several people or entities according to a set criteria.

Q

quick ratio. As used in this book, it is the total of unsecured debts divided by one year's disposable income. In financial analysis, it is cash, marketable securities, and accounts receivable divided by current liabilities.

R

reaffirmation agreement. An agreement signed by a bankruptcy petitioner stating that he or she will continue paying a given debt owed to a creditor after the bankruptcy is completed. This is normally done for one of three reasons: (1) a sense of moral obligation; (2) to keep access to credit offered by a creditor (as in credit cards); or, (3) to keep collateral—such as a vehicle—which is subject to repossession.

real estate. Land with or without buildings on it (also called *real property*).

repossession. The taking of property that has been pledged as security or as collateral for the repayment of a loan. A repossession can be done with or without a court order.

right of offset. The ability of a person or business that holds another's money (like a bank) to apply the money being held to a debt that is owed to that person or business. For example, a bank can apply money from your account to an overdrawn check on your account.

S

secured debt. A debt that is backed or secured by a claim on property. Examples are mortgages, claims against vehicles, or accounts receivable.

security interest. The claim or lien on an item of property or an asset created by an agreement between a debtor and a creditor. This is different from a judgment lien or a tax lien created by a court or action of law.

senior lien. A lien that must be paid or satisfied first when an item of property has more than one claim against it. An example is a first mortgage where there is a first and second mortgage.

service of lawsuit papers. The delivery of a complaint or other lawsuit papers. This starts a lawsuit against the defendant. Lawsuit papers can be served by certified mail, a sheriff or other legal officer, or by a process server.

sole proprietorship. A business owned or operated by an individual that is not incorporated on part of a partnership.

statement of intentions. A declaration in a bankruptcy petition stating how secured and other debts will be treated.

statutory lien. A claim created by a statute or operation of the law. A common example is a tax lien against property.

stockholder. One who owns an interest in a corporation.

subprime loan or subprime mortgage. A loan or mortgage to a person whose credit record causes him or her to need to pay a higher interest rate or who would normally be turned down when applying for a loan or mortgage.

T

tax lien. A claim by a tax authority against property because of an overdue tax debt or obligation.

trade creditors. An individual or entity that has provided credit to a business.

trustee. A person or entity that has a claim on property for the benefit of a third party. Common examples are a trustee in connection with a home mortgage or a bankruptcy trustee. In bankruptcy, the term is used to refer to the bankruptcy trustee.

U

unsecured debt. A debt not secured by an interest in an item of property or an asset.

unsecured loan. A promise by an individual or entity to pay a debt that is not backed by a security interest.

W

wage earner plan (or wage earner bankruptcy). Another name for Chapter 13 bankruptcy.

wage garnishment. The taking of all or part of a debtor's wages for the benefit of a creditor. The employer takes the wages earned by the debtor and sends them to the creditor. This is done for private nongovernmental creditors only after a money judgment. Government creditors can have a wage garnishment put in place without a court order.

wild card (or wild card exemption). The right to protect from creditors or a bankruptcy trustee any item of property up to a set dollar value.

workout (or workout program). An arrangement to pay a debt after the debt has gone into default.

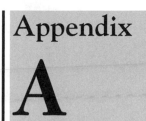

PERSONAL AND BUSINESS BUDGETING

Personal Budget—Family of Four

This budget is based on household operating income. To get household operating income, you would take after-tax income and deduct:

1. child support and spousal support payments;

2. student loans and criminal restitution payments; and,

3. tuition and living expenses for family members at colleges and private schools.

Percentage of household operating income spent on each category

Housing *(includes mortgage payments, rent, heat, electricity, etc.)*	20–40%
Food	10–20%
Transportation *(includes vehicle payments, gas, oil, vehicle insurance, bus fare, saving for a replacement vehicle, etc.)*	15–20%
Clothing	5–15%

Recreation, religious institution, and charitable giving   5–20%
(*includes vacations*)

Medical, dental, and personal care   5–10%
(*if you have a serious medical problem, this could be a lot higher*)

The astute reader will note that these percentages can add up to more than 100%. This means that to live without resorting to borrowing, a family must trade off high spending in one area with low spending in other areas.

This sample budget does not have a category for the repayment of credit cards and personal loans. If your monthly debt payment is too large a percentage of your household operating income, you must cut back on spending in other areas or face the real possibility of eventual default.

Debt

How much debt is too much? The traditional rule of thumb is that your debt repayments should not exceed one-third of the money you have left over after subtracting the money you spend in the previously listed categories from your household operating income.

Another traditional general guideline is that your total general debts—other than your house and car loans—should not be larger than 20% of your household operating income for the year.

Business Budget

What a given business needs to spend in different areas—office space, employees, advertising, supplies, transportation, etc.—varies so much from business to business that a guideline for expenditures in each different area cannot be given. For example, an accountant is likely to have high expenses for office space, supplies, employees, and ongoing education, but might have a low percentage of his or her business expenses directed toward advertising and transportation. On the other hand, a plumber might have high expenses for advertising and transportation, but spend little on office space.

However, despite these variations, most small business owners use a general guideline of trying to limit the sum of these business expenses to 50% of their business income.

Federal and State-Specific Bankruptcy Exemptions

Throughout the text of this book, there are several references to various exemptions one can take in bankruptcy. These are dollar amounts and limits on certain items (e.g., your home, vehicles, etc.) that cannot be used to pay your creditors. Listed in this appendix are both federal exemptions and any state-specific ones. On pages 190–191 there is a list of states that allow you to choose between using your state's exemptions or the federal exemptions.

The bankruptcy exemption law was changed in 2005 to control what exemption laws are used when people move between states shortly before they file for bankruptcy. If you have lived in the state you file for bankruptcy in for less than 730 days (two years), you must use your prior state's exemptions. Count out the 180 days before the 730-day period, and use the exemptions for the state you were living in for the majority of that 180-day period.

There are problems with the 180-day counting program set up by Congress. Sometimes a debtor is not domiciled in any state because he or she has been traveling, or the prior state will only allow residents of that state to use its exemptions. In these cases, the debtor will use the federal exemptions.

If your bankruptcy falls under the 730-day rule, you should consult with an attorney.

Federal Bankruptcy Exemptions

Please note that the dollar amounts listed as follows change every year. Also, the following information is not intended to provide legal advice, but rather only to provide you with general guidelines. Make sure you discuss your individual case with an attorney to see which exemptions you would qualify for.

Homestead up to:	$20,200
Motor Vehicle up to:	$3,225
Personal Property up to:	$525 of value per item, up to $10,775 total
Tools of Trade up to:	$2,025
Jewelry up to:	$1,350
Wild Card:	$1,075 for any property, plus up to $10,125 of any unused amount of the homestead exemption.

Federal exemptions can be used as an alternative to state exemptions by residents of the following states:

Arkansas

Connecticut

District of Columbia

Hawaii

Massachusetts

Michigan

Minnesota

New Hampshire

New Jersey

New Mexico

Pennsylvania

Rhode Island

Texas

Vermont

Washington

Wisconsin

State Exemptions

Alabama

Homestead up to:	$5,000 (160 acres maximum)
Motor Vehicle up to:	Included in personal property
Personal Property up to:	$3,000
Tools of Trade	Military equipment
Wild Card:	$3,000

Alaska

Homestead up to:	$67,500
Motor Vehicle up to:	$3,750 (if the value of the vehicle is not over $25,000)
Personal Property up to:	$3,000
Tools of Trade up to:	$2,800

Jewelry up to: $1,250

Pets up to: $1,250

Arizona

Homestead up to: $150,000
                            Limited to $136,875 if property acquired
                            within 1,215 days of filing bankruptcy

Motor Vehicle up to: $5,000 ($10,000 if physically
                            disabled)

Personal Property up to: $4,000 of assorted furniture, furnish-
                            ings, and appliances

                            $500 of clothing

                            $250 of a personal library

Tools of Trade up to: $2,500

Jewelry up to: $1,000 for engagement and wedding rings

Pets up to: $500

Arkansas

Homestead up to: Head of household may claim any amount if
                            property is under one-fourth of an acre in a city
                            or under eighty acres elsewhere. If the property is
                            between one-fourth and one acre in the city, or
                            80–160 acres elsewhere, the exemption is $2,500.

Motor Vehicle up to: None

Personal Property up to: $200 if single, $500 if married. No limit on the value of clothing.

Tools of Trade up to: None

California

Note: *There are two options for bankruptcy exemptions in California. The two systems cannot be mixed.*

Option 1.

Homestead up to: $50,000 if single

$75,000 if a member of the family and no one else is claiming a homestead

$150,000 if 65 or older or disabled; single, 55 or older, and earn less than $15,000 per year; or, married, 55 or older, and earn less than $20,000 per year

Motor Vehicle up to: $2,550

Personal Property up to: All food, clothing, appliances, furnishings, and health aids. Home building materials up to $2,425.

Tools of Trade up to: $6,750

Jewelry: up to: $6,750

Option 2.

Homestead up to: $20,725

Motor Vehicle up to: $3,300

Personal Property up to:	Clothing, household goods, appliances, furnishings, animals, books, musical instruments, and crops up to $525 per item
Tools of Trade up to:	$2,075
Jewelry: up to:	$1,150
Wild Card:	$1,100 and any unused portion of the homestead exemption can be used to protect personal property

Colorado

Homestead up to:	$45,000. Property must be occupied at the time of filing
Motor Vehicle up to:	$3,000. Up to $6,000 if elderly or disabled
Personal Property up to:	Clothing up to $1,500
	Health aids
	Household goods up to $3,000
	Food and fuel up to $600
	$1,500 of books and pictures
Tools of Trade up to:	Stocks in trade, supplies, fixtures, machines, tools, maps, equipment, and books up to $10,000
	$3,000 for the library of a professional
	$25,000 of farm materials and animals for a farmer
Jewelry up to:	$1,000

Connecticut

Homestead up to:	$75,000
Motor Vehicle up to:	$1,500
Personal Property up to:	100% of food, clothing, health aids, appliances, furniture, bedding
Tools of Trade up to:	100% of military equipment, tools, books, instruments, and farm animals necessary for one's occupation
Jewelry up to:	100% of wedding and engagement rings
Wild Card:	$1,000 of any property

Delaware

Homestead up to:	$50,000 for principal residence
Motor Vehicle up to:	$15,000
Personal Property up to:	General exemption per person—clothing, jewelry, books, family pictures, piano, school books, and family library
Tools of Trade up to:	$15,000 minus the amount used for a motor vehicle.

Note: *Total exemption for motor vehicle and personal property may not exceed $25,000 per person.*

District of Columbia

Homestead up to:	Unlimited so long as it is used as debtor's residence
	Limited to $136,875 if property acquired within 1,215 days of filing bankruptcy
Motor Vehicle up to:	$2,575
Personal Property up to:	$425 per item for household goods, animals, clothing, crops, and musical instruments, up to $8,625 total
	$400 for family pictures and family library
Tools of Trade up to:	$1,625

Note: *These exemptions can be claimed by residents of D.C. or by those who earn the major portion of their income in D.C.*

Florida

Homestead up to:	Unlimited value for one-half acre in the city or 160 acres elsewhere
	Limited to $136,875 if the property was acquired within 1,215 days of filing for bankruptcy
Motor Vehicle up to:	$1,000
Personal Property up to:	100% of health aids
	$4,000 of personal property if homestead exemption is not used; otherwise, $1,000 of personal property
Tools of Trade up to:	Included in personal property exemption

Georgia

Homestead up to:	$10,000
Motor Vehicle up to:	$3,500
Personal Property up to:	$300 per household item, up to $5,000 total
Tools of Trade up to:	$1,500
Jewelry up to:	$500
Wild Card:	$600 to protect any property and up to $5,000 of any unused portion of the homestead exemption

Hawaii

Homestead up to:	$30,000 for heads of household or people over 65
	$20,000 for anyone else
	Property cannot exceed one acre
Motor Vehicle up to:	$2,575
Personal Property up to:	All necessary household goods
Tools of Trade up to:	All tools needed for livelihood
Jewelry up to:	$1,000

Idaho

Homestead up to:	$50,000
Motor Vehicle up to:	$3,000

Personal Property up to: $500 per household good, up to $5,000 total

Tools of Trade up to: $1,500 and all arms and equipment kept by peace officers and military personnel

Jewelry up to: $1,000

Illinois

Homestead up to: $15,000

Motor Vehicle up to: $2,400

Personal Property up to: All necessary clothes, health aids, school books, and Bibles

$4,000 of other personal property

Tools of Trade up to: $1,500

Indiana

Homestead up to: $15,000

Motor Vehicle up to: Included in personal property

Personal Property up to: $8,000 of real estate or tangible personal property

$300 of intangible personal property

Tools of Trade up to: National Guard uniforms and equipment

Iowa

Homestead up to:	Unlimited value, but property can be no larger than one-half an acre in a town or 40 acres elsewhere
	Limited to $136,875 if property was acquired within 1,215 days of filing for bankruptcy
Motor Vehicle up to:	No specific exemption
Personal Property up to:	$7,000, plus $1,000 of a personal library
Tools of Trade up to:	$10,000 of nonfarming equipment
	$10,000 of farming equipment and livestock

Kansas

Homestead up to:	Unlimited value, but property can be no larger than 1 acre in town or 160 acres elsewhere
	Limited to $136,875 if property was acquired within 1,215 days of filing for bankruptcy
Motor Vehicle up to:	$20,000. Unlimited if designed for a disabled person.
Personal Property up to:	All household goods, food, fuel, and clothing to last one year
Tools of Trade up to:	$7,500, plus National Guard uniforms and equipment
Jewelry up to:	$1,000

Kentucky

Homestead up to:	$5,000
Motor Vehicle up to:	$2,500
Personal Property up to:	$3,000 of household goods, including jewelry and health aids
Tools of Trade up to:	$3,000 of farm equipment and livestock
	$300 of nonfarming tools
	$2,500 for a vehicle for a mechanic, a mechanical or electrical equipment servicer, or a professional.
	$1,000 for a library and office equipment for a professional
Wild Card:	$1,000 of any property

Louisiana

Homestead up to:	$25,000
	Limited to 5 acres in a city and 200 acres elsewhere
Motor Vehicle up to:	$7,500
Personal Property up to:	Unlimited
Tools of Trade up to:	All necessary tools, books, instruments, a vehicle, and a utility trailer needed for work
Jewelry up to:	$5,000 for wedding and engagement rings

Maine

Homestead up to:	$35,000
	$70,000 if caring for dependents
	$70,000 if age 60 or older or disabled
Motor Vehicle up to:	$5,000
Personal Property up to:	$750 of certain kitchen appliances and supplies, health aids, and jewelry
	$200 per item of personal property, farm supplies to harvest one season's crops
	$400 of any property
Tools of Trade up to:	$5,000

Maryland

Homestead up to:	$5,000
Motor Vehicle up to:	None. Can use wild card money to protect.
Personal Property up to:	$1,000 of clothing, household goods, and pets.
Tools of Trade up to:	$5,000
Wild Card:	$5,000

Massachusetts

Homestead up to:	$500,000
	Limited to $136,875 if property acquired within 1,215 days of filing bankruptcy

Motor Vehicle up to:	$700
Personal Property up to:	Necessary clothing, beds, bedding, heating unit
	$200 of books
	$3,000 of furniture
	$200 per month for rent if no homestead exemption is used
	$300 for food
Tools of Trade up to:	$500, $500 of materials you designed, plus $500 for a boat and fisherman's equipment
	All military equipment

Michigan

Homestead up to:	$30,000
	$45,000 if disabled or age 65 or older
Motor Vehicle up to:	$2,775
Personal Property up to:	$3,000 in household goods, furniture, books, and jewelry up to $450 for each item
	All necessary clothing
Tools of Trade up to:	$2,000

Minnesota

Homestead up to:	$300,000
	$500,000 if primarily used for agriculture
	May not exceed one-half acre in a city or 160 acres elsewhere
	Limited to $136,875 if property acquired within 1,215 days of filing bankruptcy
Motor Vehicle up to:	$2,000
	$20,000 for a vehicle modified to serve a disabled person
Personal Property up to:	$9,000
Tools of Trade up to:	$5,000
	$13,000 for farm implements used in farming
Jewelry up to:	$1,225 in wedding rings

Mississippi

Homestead up to:	$75,000. Limited to 160 acres.
Motor Vehicle up to:	Included under personal property
Personal Property up to:	$10,000
Tools of Trade up to:	Included under personal property

Missouri

Homestead up to:	$15,000 for real property
	$5,000 for a mobile home
Motor Vehicle up to:	$3,000
Personal Property up to:	$3,000 of clothing, household goods, and books
	Health aids
	$1,250 of any property for the head of household plus $350 per unmarried dependent under age 18 or disabled
Jewelry up to:	$500
	$1,500 for a wedding ring
Tools of Trade up to:	$3,000

Montana

Homestead up to:	$250,000
	Limited to $136,875 if property acquired within 1,215 days of filing bankruptcy
Motor Vehicle up to:	$2,500
Personal Property up to:	$4,500 in household goods, up to $600 per item
	Health aids
Tools of Trade up to:	$3,000 and all military equipment

Nebraska

Homestead up to:	$12,500
	No more than two contiguous lots in a city or 160 acres elsewhere
Motor Vehicle up to:	Included under personal property
Personal Property up to:	$1,500 in household goods and furnishings
	$2,500 in personal property
Tools of Trade up to:	$2,400

Nevada

Homestead up to:	$550,000
	Limited to $136,875 if property acquired within 1,215 days of filing bankruptcy
Motor Vehicle up to:	$15,000
	Unlimited if equipped for the disabled
Personal Property up to:	$12,000 in necessary household goods
	$5,000 of books and jewelry
	Health aids and 1 gun
Tools of Trade up to:	$10,000
	$4,500 in farm equipment
	$4,500 in mining equipment
	All military equipment

New Hampshire

Homestead up to:	$100,000
Motor Vehicle up to:	$4,000
Personal Property up to:	$3,500 in furniture and most other household goods
	Necessary clothing
	$800 of books
	Some farm animals and hay
Tools of Trade up to:	$5,000
	Military equipment and one cow, horse, or yoke of oxen when needed for farming
Jewelry up to:	$500
Wild Card:	$1,000 of other property, plus up to $7,000 in any unused exemption amounts

New Jersey

Homestead up to:	None
Motor Vehicle up to:	Included under personal property
Personal Property up to:	$1,000 of household goods and furniture
	Clothing
	$1,000 in other personal property
Tools of Trade up to:	None

New Mexico

Homestead up to:	$60,000
Motor Vehicle up to:	$4,000
Personal Property up to:	All household goods
	$500 of personal property
Tools of Trade up to:	$1,500
Jewelry up to:	$2,500

New York

Homestead up to:	$50,000
Motor Vehicle up to:	$2,400
Personal Property up to:	Most household goods
	$50 of books
	$35 watch
	$450 of domestic animals
	Total of personal property may not exceed $5,000
Tools of Trade up to:	$600
Wild Card:	$2,500 cash in lieu of homestead and personal property exemptions

North Carolina

Homestead up to:	$18,500
Motor Vehicle up to:	$3,500

Personal Property up to: $5,000, plus $1,000 per dependent (up to $4,000)

Tools of Trade up to: $2,000

Wild Card: $5,000 of unused homestead exemption can be used to protect other property

North Dakota

Homestead up to: $80,000

Motor Vehicle up to: $1,200

$32,000 if modified for a disabled owner

Personal Property up to: Clothing, food and fuel for one year; books up to $100; crops and grains raised on the debtor's land; and pictures

The head of a family not claiming crops may claim $5,000 of any property, or up to $1,000 of furniture, $1,500 of books and musical instruments, $1,000 of a library or professional tools, $1,000 of tools for a mechanic, and $4,500 of farm implements and livestock

A single person may claim $2,500 of personal property

Tools of Trade up to: Included under personal property

Wild Card: $7,500 if homestead exemption is not used

Ohio

Homestead up to:	$5,000
Motor Vehicle up to:	$1,000
Personal Property up to:	Household goods, furnishings, books, animals, musical instruments, firearms, and crops, not to exceed $2,000 (or $1,500 if homestead exemption is claimed)
	$200 per item of clothing, beds, and bedding
	$300 per item for a cooking unit and refrigerator
	Health aids
	$400 of any property
	$400 of cash
Tools of Trade up to:	$750
Jewelry up to:	$1,500 total if claiming homestead exemption and $2,000 total if not, up to $200 for each piece

Oklahoma

Homestead up to:	Unlimited if property is on one acre in a city or 160 acres elsewhere
	$5,000 if homestead is in a city and used for both business and residence, and the residence is not at least 75% of the property
	$136,875 if property acquired within 1,215 days of filing bankruptcy

Motor Vehicle up to:	$7,500
Personal Property up to:	$4,000 of clothing; all furniture, books, portraits, pictures, health aids; one year of food; two bridles, two saddles, one hundred chickens, twenty sheep, ten hogs, five cows, two horses, and forage for livestock to last one year
Tools of Trade up to:	$10,000
Jewelry up to:	$3,000 of wedding and anniversary rings

Oregon

Homestead up to:	$30,000 on land you own (up to $39,600 if jointly owned)
	$20,000 for a mobile home on land you do not own (up to $27,000 if jointly owned)
	$23,000 for a mobile home on land you do own (up to $30,000 if jointly owned)
Motor Vehicle up to:	$2,150
Personal Property up to:	$1,800 of clothing, jewelry, and personal items
	$3,000 of household items, furniture, utensils, televisions, and radios
	Health aids
	$1,000 of domestic animals and poultry
	$600 of books, pictures, and musical instruments
	$400 of any personal property not already covered under any other exemption
Tools of Trade up to:	$3,000

Pennsylvania

Homestead up to:	None
Motor Vehicle up to:	Included under personal property
Personal Property up to:	$300 of any property
	Clothing, Bibles, and school books and uniforms
Tools of Trade up to:	None
Wild Card:	$300

Rhode Island

Homestead up to:	$300,000
	Limited to $136,875 if property acquired within 1,215 days of filing bankruptcy
Motor Vehicle up to:	$10,000
Personal Property up to:	$8,600 of household goods and furniture
	Clothing
	$300 of books
Tools of Trade up to:	$1,200
	Practicing professional's library
Jewelry up to:	$1,000

South Carolina

Homestead up to:	$50,000
Motor Vehicle up to:	$1,200

Personal Property up to:	$2,500 of household furnishings, clothing, books, animals, and musical instruments
Tools of Trade up to:	$750
Jewelry up to:	$500
Wild Card:	$1,000 of property if homestead exemption is not claimed

South Dakota

Homestead up to:	Unlimited. Must not exceed one acre in a town or 160 acres or less elsewhere.
	Unlimited for mobile homes
	Limited to $136,875 if property acquired within 1,215 days of filing for bankruptcy.
Motor Vehicle up to:	Included under personal property
Personal Property up to:	$6,000 for the head of the family
	$4,000 if single
	$200 for books
	Clothing
Tools of Trade up to:	Included under personal property

Tennessee

Homestead up to:	$5,000 for single person
	$7,500 for married couple
	$12,000 for single person over the age of 62
	$20,000 for married couple where one person is over the age of 62

$25,000 for married couple where both persons are over the age of 62, and for a single person with custody of one or more minor children

Motor Vehicle up to:	Included under personal property
Personal Property up to:	$4,000

Clothing, storage containers, school books, pictures, portraits, and Bible

Tools of Trade up to: $1,900

Texas

Homestead up to: Unlimited, but cannot exceed ten acres in a town or one hundred acres elsewhere (two hundred acres for a family.)

Limited to $136,875 if property was acquired within 1,215 days of filing for bankruptcy

Motor Vehicle up to: One motor vehicle

See limitation under personal property.

Personal Property up to: Home furnishings, food, and clothing

Two firearms, sports equipment, two horses or mules with riding equipment, twelve cattle, sixty other livestock, 120 fowl, feed for the animals, and household pets.

Note: *$30,000 limit for total value of vehicles, personal property, owed wages, and tools of the trade. ($60,000 limit for the head of a family.)*

Tools of Trade up to: Tools, books, and equipment, including motor vehicles, boats, farming, and ranch vehicles, and instruments used in a trade or profession.

See limitation under personal property.

Jewelry: $7,500

See limitation under personal property.

Utah

Homestead up to: $20,000 if primary residence

$5,000 if not primary residence

Motor Vehicle up to: $2,500

Personal Property up to: All clothing, but for jewelry and furs

Refrigerator, freezer, stove, washer, dryer, sewing machine, needed health aides, twelve months of food, beds and bedding

$500 of sofas, chairs, and related furnishings

$500 of dining and kitchen tables and chairs

$500 of animals, books, and musical instruments

$500 of heirlooms or other items of sentimental value

Tools of Trade up to: $3,500 of business tools, books, and implements

Military property of a National Guard member

Vermont

Homestead up to:	$75,000
Motor Vehicle up to:	$2,500
Personal Property up to:	$2,500 of clothing, goods, furnishings, appliances, books, musical instruments, animals, and crops
	$5,000 of growing crops
	$400 of any property
Tools of Trade up to:	$5,000
Jewelry up to:	$500 and wedding ring
Wildcard:	$$400 of any property, plus up to $7,000 of unused amounts of certain exemptions

Virginia

Homestead up to:	$5,000 plus $500 per dependent
Motor Vehicle up to:	$2,000
Personal Property up to:	$1,000 of clothing
	$5,000 of household furnishings
	$5,000 of family portraits and heirlooms
	Health aids
Tools of Trade up to:	$10,000 of tools, books, instruments, equipment, and machines necessary for use in occupation or trade
	For a farmer: two plows, one wagon or cart, one pair of horses, $1,000 of fertilizer, $3,000 of a tractor

	Arms, uniforms, and equipment of someone in the military
Jewelry up to:	Wedding and engagement rings
Wild Card:	$2,000 for disabled veterans (40% or more disabled) with a service-related disability

Washington

Homestead up to:	$125,000
Motor Vehicle up to:	$2,500
Personal Property up to:	$1,000 of clothing and jewelry
	$2,700 of household goods
	$1,500 of books and private libraries
	$2,000 of any property (but no more than $200 in cash, stocks, or bonds)
Tools of Trade up to:	$5,000
Jewelry up to:	$1,000

West Virginia

Homestead up to:	$25,000
Motor Vehicle up to:	$2,400
Personal Property up to:	$8,000 of clothing, household goods, furnishings, appliances, books, musical instruments, animals, and crops, but no more than $400 per item
	$1,000 of personal property belonging to the head of the household

Tools of Trade up to:	$1,500
Jewelry up to:	$1,000
Wild Card:	$800 plus unused amount of homestead exemption for personal property

Wisconsin

Homestead up to:	$40,000
Motor Vehicle up to:	$1,200, plus any unused portion of the personal property exemption
Personal Property up to:	$5,000 of household goods, including jewelry, sporting goods, and animals
	$1,000 in deposit accounts
Tools of Trade up to:	$7,500

Wyoming

Homestead up to:	$10,000
Mobile Home Homestead up to:	$6,000
Motor Vehicle up to:	$2,400
Personal Property up to:	$1,000 of clothing and wedding rings
	$2,000 of furniture and other household items
	School books, pictures, and a Bible
Tools of Trade or Professional Library up to:	$2,000

Consumer Credit Counseling Services

National Foundation of Credit Counseling
801 Roeder Road, Suite 900
Silver Spring, MD 20910
301-589-5600
800-388-2227
www.nfcc.org

Local Consumer Credit Counseling Services

Alabama

CCCS of Alabama, Inc.
777 South Lawrence Street, Suite 101
Montgomery, AL 36104
334-265-8545
800-662-6119
www.budgethelp.com

CCCS of Mobile-Family Counseling Center of Mobile, Inc.
705 Oak Circle Drive, East
Mobile, AL 36609
251-602-0011
888-880-1416
www.cccsmobile.org

**CCCS of Central Alabama
(Division of Gateway)**
1401-20th Street South, Suite 100
Birmingham, AL 35205-4913
205-251-1572
888-260-2227
www.gway.org

Alaska

CCCS of Alaska
208 East 4th Avenue
Anchorage, AK 99501
907-279-6501
www.cccsofak.com

Arizona

**CCCS – Central Phoenix Branch
Money Management International**
722 East Osborn Road, Suite 210
Phoenix, AZ 85014
866-889-9347
www.moneymanagement.org

**CCCS – Flaggstaff Branch
Money Management International**
2615 North 4th Street, Suite 2
Flagstaff, AZ 86004
866-889-9347
www.moneymanagement.org

**CCCS – Glendale Branch
Money Management International**
17235 North 75th Avenue
Suite C-125
Glendale, AZ 85308
866-889-9347
www.moneymanagement.org

**CCCS – Mesa Branch
Money Management International**
1234 South Power Road, Suite 100
Mesa, AZ 85206
866-889-9347
www.moneymanagement.org

**CCCS – North Phoenix Branch
Money Management International**
1717 Beast Bell Road, Suite 7
Phoenix, AZ 85308
866-889-9347
www.moneymanagement.org

**CCCS – Prescott Branch
Money Management International**
1215 Gail Gardener Way, Suite B
Prescott, AZ 86305
866-889-9347
www.moneymanagement.org

CCCS – Tempe Branch
Money Management International
950 West Elliott Road, Suite 122
Tempe, AZ 85284
866-889-9347
www.moneymanagement.org

CCCS – Tuscon Branch
Money Management International
5515 East Grant Road, Suite 211
Tucson, AZ 85712
866-889-9347
www.moneymanagement.org

CCCS – Tucson Branch
Money Management International
4732 North Oracle Road, Suite 217
Tucson, AZ 85707
866-889-9347
www.moneymanagement.org

CCCS – Yuma Branch
Money Management International
2450 South Fourth Avenue, Suite 500
Yuma, AZ 85364
866-889-9347
www.moneymanagement.org

Arkansas

CCCS – El Dorado Branch
Money Management International
202 North Washington, Suite 101
El Dorado, AR 71730
866-889-9347
www.moneymanagement.org

Credit Counseling of Arkansas, Inc.
P.O. Box 10290
1111 Zion Road
Fayetteville, AR 72703
479-521-8877
800-889-4916
www.ccoacares.com

Family Service Agency - CCCS
628 West Broadway, Suite 203
North Little Rock, AR 72114
501-753-0202
800-255-2227
www.helpingfamilies.org

California

ByDesign Financial Solutions
6001 Washington Boulevard
2nd Floor
Los Angeles, CA 90040
323-890-9500
800-750-2227
www.bydesignsolutions.org

CCCS – Berkeley Branch
Money Management International
2140 Shattuck Avenue, Suite 1208
Berkeley, CA 94704
866-889-9347
www.moneymanagement.org

CCCS – Chula Vista Branch
Money Management International
730 Broadway, Suite 200
Pacific Western Bank
Chula Vista, CA 91911
866-889-9347
www.moneymanagement.org

CCCS – Concord Branch
Money Management International
1070 Concord Avenue, Suite 105
Concord, CA 94520
866-889-9347
www.moneymanagement.org

CCCS – Fremont Branch
Money Management International
3100 Mowry Avenue, Suite 403-A
Fremont, CA 94538
866-889-9347
www.moneymanagement.org

CCCS of Kern & Tulare Counties
5300 Lennox Avenue, Suite 200
Bakersfield, CA 93309
661-324-9628
www.californiaccccs.org

CCCS of the North Coast
1309 11th Street, Suite 104
Arcata, CA 95521
707-822-8536
800-762-1811
www.cccsnojuggle.org

CCCS – Oakland Branch
Money Management International
7677 Oakport Street, Suite 210
Oakland, CA 94621
866-889-9347
www.moneymanagement.org

CCCS – Oceanside Branch
Money Management International
1949 Avenida Del Oro, Suite 106
Oceanside, CA 92056
866-889-9347
www.moneymanagement.org

CCCS – San Diego Branch
Money Management International
2650 Camino del Rio North, Suite 209
San Diego, CA 92108
866-889-9347
www.moneymanagement.org

CCCS of San Francisco
595 Market Street, 15th Floor
San Francisco, CA 94105
415-788-0288
800-777-7526
www.cccssf.org

CCCS of Santa Clara & Ventura County, Inc.
80 North Wood Road, Suite 308
Camarillo, CA 93010
805-383-7700
800-540-2227
www.gotdebt.org

CCCS, Twin Cities
718-B Bridge Street
Yuba City, CA 95991
Phone: (530) 674-9729
Appointments: (530) 674-9729
Fax: (530) 674-2938
Email: alicev@mako.com

Consumer Credit Counseling Service of Orange County
1920 Old Tustin Avenue
Santa Ana, CA 92705
714-547-2227
www.cccsoc.org

Springboard Non-Profit Consumer Credit Management
4351 Latham Street
Riverside, CA 92501
951-781-0114
800-947-3752
www.credit.org

Colorado

CCCS – Denver Aurora Branch
Money Management International
10065 East Harvard Avenue
Suite 210
Denver, CO 80231
866-889-9347
www.moneymanagement.org

CCCS – Denver Downtown Branch
Money Management International
600 17th Street, Suite 2800 South
South Denver, CO 80202
866-889-9347
www.moneymanagement.org

CCCS – Grand Junction Branch
Money Management International
225 North 5th Street, Suite 820
Grand Junction, CO 81502
866-889-9347
www.moneymanagement.org

CCCS – Highlands Ranch Branch
Money Management International
7120 East County Line Road
Highlands Ranch, CO 80126
866-889-9347

www.moneymanagement.org

CCCS – Jeffco Schools Branch
Money Management International
355 Union
Lakewood, CO 80229
866-889-9347

www.moneymanagement.org

CCCS of Northern Colorado &
Southeast Wyoming
1247 Riverside Avenue
Fort Collins, CO 80524-3258
970-229-0695

www.cccsnc.org

CCCS – Westminster Branch
Money Management International
9101 Harlan Street, Suite 150
Westminster, CO 80030
866-889-9347

www.moneymanagement.org

Connecticut

CCCS – East Hartford Branch
Money Management International
225 Pitkin Street, Suite 300
East Hartford, CT 06108
866-889-9347

www.moneymanagement.org

CCCS – Milford Branch
Money Management International
61 Cherry Street, Building H, Suite
C-2
Milford, CT 06460
866-889-9347

www.moneymanagement.org

CCCS – North Franklin Branch
Money Management International
627 Route 32
North Franklin, CT 06254
866-889-9347

www.moneymanagement.org

District of Columbia

CCCS – Washington D.C. Branch
Money Management International
1250 Connecticut Avenue, NW, Suite 48
Washington, DC 2036
866-889-9347

www.moneymanagement.org

Florida

CCCS of Brevard (A Division of the Family Counseling Center)
507 North Harbor City Boulevard
Melbourne, FL 32935
321-259-1070
www.cccsbrevard.org

CCCS of Central Florida and the Florida Gulf Coast, Inc.
3670 Maguire Boulevard, Suite 103
Orlando, FL 32803
407-895-8886
800-741-7040
www.cccsfl.org

CCCS of Jacksonville (Family Foundations)
1639 Atlantic Boulevard
Jacksonville, FL 32207
904-396-4846
888-297-1929
www.fcsjax.org

CCCS of Mid-Florida, Inc.
1539 NE 22nd Avenue
Ocala, FL 33470
352-867-1865
800-245-1865
www.cccsmidflorida.com

CCCS of West Florida, Inc.
14 Palafox Place
Pensacola, FL 32502
850-434-0268
www.cccswfl.org

Georgia

CCCS of Greater Atlanta, Inc.
100 Edgewood Avenue NW, Suite 1800
Atlanta, GA 30303
404-527-7630
800-251-2227
www.cccsinc.org

CCCS of Middle Georgia, Inc.
277 Martin Luther King Boulevard, Suite 202
Macon, GA 31201
478-745-6197
800-446-7123
www.cccsmacon.org

CCCS of the Savannah Area, Inc.
7505 Waters Avenue, Park South, Suite C-11
Savannah, GA 31406
912-691-2227
800-821-4040
www.cccssavannah.org

CCCS of Southwest Georgia
409 North Jackson Street
Albany, GA 31701
229-883-0909
800-309-3358
www.cccsalbany.org

CCCS of West Georgia/East Alabama
1350 15th Avenue
P.O. Box 1825
Columbus, GA 31902
706-327-3239

Hawaii

CCCS of Hawaii
1164 Bishop Street, Suite 1614
Honolulu, HI 96813
808-532-3225
www.cccsofhawaii.org

Idaho

CCCS – Coeur d'Alene Branch Money Management International
1801 Lincoln Way, Suite 6
Coeur d'Alene, ID 83814
866-889-9347
www.moneymanagement.org

CCCS of Northern Idaho
1113 Main Street
Lewiston, ID 83501
208-746-0127
800-556-0127
www.cccsnid.org

Illinois

CCCS – Central Illinois Branch Money Management International
The Commerce Building
416 Main Street, Suite 920
Peoria, IL 60602
866-889-9347
www.moneymanagement.org

CCCS – Chicago/ Downtown Branch Money Management International
70 East Lake Street, Suite 1115
Chicago, IL 60601
866-889-9347
www.moneymanagement.org

CCCS of Elgin (A Division of Family Service Association/Greater Elgin Area)
22 South Spring Street
Elgin, IL 60120
847-695-3680
www.fsaelgin.org/cccs.htm

CCCS – Glen Ellyn Branch
Money Management International
1200 Roosevelt Road, Suite 108
Glen Ellyn, IL 60137
866-889-9347
www.moneymanagement.org

CCCS of McHenry County, Inc.
400 Russel Court
P.O. Box 885
Woodstock, IL 60098
815-338-5757
www.illinoiscccs.org

CCCS of North Central Illinois
1003 Martin Luther King Drive
Bloomington, IL 61701
309-820-3501
800-615-3022
www.chestnut.org

CCCS – Oak Park Branch
Money Management International
1515 North Harlem, Suite 205
Oak Park, IL 60302
866-889-9347
www.moneymanagement.org

CCCS – Rockford Branch
Money Management International
129 South Phelps Avenue, Suite 811
Rockford, IL 61108
866-889-9347
www.moneymanagement.org

CCCS – Rolling Meadows Branch
Money Management International
3601 Algonquin Road, Suite 230
Rolling Meadows, IL 60008
866-889-9347
www.moneymanagement.org

CCCS – Tinley Park Branch
Money Management International
16860 South Oak Park Avenue, Suite 230
Tinley Park, IL 60477
866-889-9347
www.moneymanagement.org

Family Counseling Service/ CCCS of Aurora
70 South River Street, Suite 2
Aurora, IL 60506
630-844-3327
800-349-1451
www.aurorafcs.org

Indiana

CCCS of Lafayette (A Division of Family Service, Inc.)
615 N 18th Street
Howarth Center, Suite 201
Lafayette, IN 47904
765-423-5361
800-875-5361
www.fsilafayette.org

CCCS of Northeastern Indiana
4105 West Jefferson Boulevard
Fort Wayne, IN 46804
260-432-8200
800-432-0420
www.financialhope.org

CCCS of Northwest Indiana
3637 Grant Street
Gary, IN 46408
219-980-4800
800-982-4801
www.cccsnwi.org

MOMENTIVE Consumer Credit Counseling Service, Inc.
615 North Alabama Street, Suite 134
Indianapolis, IN 46204
317-266-1300
888-711-7227
www.momentive.org

Iowa

CCCS of Northeastern Iowa
1003 West Fourth Street
Waterloo, IA 50702
319-234-0661
800-714-4388
www.cccsia.org

Horizons Consumer Credit Counseling Service
819 5th Street SE
Cedar Rapids, IA 52401
319-398-3576
800-826-3574
www.horizonscccs.org

Kansas

CCCS, Inc.
1201 West Walnut
Salina, KS 67401
785-827-6731
www.kscccs.org

CCCS of Topeka (A Division of Housing and Credit Counseling, Inc.)
1195 Southwest Buchanan, Suite 101
Topeka, KS 66604
785-234-0217
800-383-0217
www.hcci-ks.org

Louisiana

CCCS – Alexandria Branch
Money Management International
1106 McArthur Drive, Suite 2
Alexandria, LA 71301
866-889-9347
www.moneymanagement.org

CCCS – Baton Rouge Branch
Money Management International
615 Chevelle Court
Baton Rouge, LA 70806
866-889-9347
www.moneymanagement.org

CCCS – Bossier City Branch
Money Management International
700 Northgate Road
Bossier City, LA 71112
866-889-9347
www.moneymanagement.org

CCCS of Greater New Orleans, Inc.
1215 Prytania Street, Suite 424
New Orleans, LA 70130
504-529-2396
800-880-2221
www.cccsno.org

CCCS – Lafayette Branch
Money Management International
117 Liberty Avenue
Lafayette, LA 70508
866-889-9347
www.moneymanagement.org

CCCS – Lake Charles Branch
Money Management International
2021 Oak Park Boulevard
Lake Charles, LA 70601
866-889-9347
www.moneymanagement.org

CCCS – Monroe Branch
Money Management International
2912 Evangeline
Monroe, LA 71201
El Dorado, AR 71730
866-889-9347
www.moneymanagement.org

CCCS – Shreveport Branch
Money Management International
8575 Business Park Drive
Shreveport, LA 71105
866-889-9347
www.moneymanagement.org

Maine

CCCS – Auburn Branch
Money Management International
250 Center Street, Suite 205
Auburn, ME 04210
866-889-9347
www.moneymanagement.org

CCCS – Bangor Branch
Money Management International
157 Park Street, Suite 34
Bangor, ME 04401
866-889-9347
www.moneymanagement.org

CCCS – Biddeford Park Branch
Money Management International
407 Alfred Road, Suite 202
Biddeford, ME 04005
866-889-9347
www.moneymanagement.org

CCCS – Hallowell Branch
Money Management International
103 Water Street, Room 204
Hallowell, ME 04347
866-889-9347
www.moneymanagement.org

CCCS – South Portland Branch
Money Management International
111 Wescott Road
P.O. Box 2560
South Portland, ME 04106
866-889-9347
www.moneymanagement.org

Maryland

CCCS – Frederick Branch
Money Management International
1003 West 7th Street, Suite 404
Frederick, MD 21701
866-889-9347
www.moneymanagement.org

CCCS of Maryland & Delaware
757 Frederick Road, 2nd Floor
Baltimore, MD 21228-3317
410-747-2050
800-642-2227
www.cccs-inc.org

CCCS – Rockville Branch
Money Management International
15847-51 Crabbs Branch Way
Rockville, MD 20855
866-889-9347
www.moneymanagement.org

Massachusetts

CCCS – Amherst Branch
Money Management International
109 Main Street, Suite 105
Amherst, MA 01002
866-889-9347
www.moneymanagement.org

CCCS – Beverly Branch
Money Management International
100 Cummings Center, Suite S-311H
Beverly, MA 01915
866-889-9347
www.moneymanagement.org

CCCS – Boston Branch
Money Management International
8 Winter Street, 7th Floor
Boston, MA 02108
866-889-9347
www.moneymanagement.org

CCCS – Lowell Branch
Money Management International
40 Central Street
Lowell, MA 01852
866-889-9347
www.moneymanagement.org

CCCS – New Bedford Branch
Money Management International
888 Purchase Street
New Bedford, MA 02740
866-889-9347
www.moneymanagement.org

CCCS – Pittsfield Branch
Money Management International
34 Depot Street
Pittsfield, MA 01202
866-889-9347
www.moneymanagement.org

CCCS – Randolph Branch
Money Management International
247 Main Street, Suite 200
Randolph, MA 02368
866-889-9347
www.moneymanagement.org

CCCS – Springfield Branch
Money Management International
59 Interstate Drive, Suite G
West Springfield, MA 01809
866-889-9347
www.moneymanagement.org

CCCS – Woburn Branch
Money Management International
800 Cummings Park, Suite 1075
Woburn, MA 01801
866-889-9347
www.moneymanagement.org

CCCS – Worcester Branch
Money Management International
74 Elm Street, 2nd Floor
Worcester, MA 01609
866-889-9347
www.moneymanagement.org

Michigan

GreenPath, Inc. d/b/a GreenPath
Debt Solutions
38505 Country Club Drive, Suite 210
Farmington Hills, MI 48331-3429
248-553-5400
866-648-8114
www.greenpath.com

Minnesota

CCCS of Duluth (Program
of Lutheran Social Service of
Minnesota)
424 West Superior Street, Suite 600
Duluth, MN 55802
218-529-2227
888-577-2227
www.lssmn.org

FamilyMeans Consumer Credit
Counseling Service
1875 Northwestern Avenue South
Stillwater, MN 55082
651-439-4840
www.familymeans.org

Missouri

CCCS of Springfield
1515 South Glenstone
Springfield, MO 65804
417-889-7474
800-882-0808
www.cccsoftheozarks.org

Montana

Rural Dynamics d/b/a CCCS of Montana
2022 Central Avenue
Great Falls, MT 59401
877-275-2227
www.cccsmt.org

Nebraska

CCCS of Nebraska, Inc.
8805 Indian Hills Drive, Suite 105
Omaha, NE 68114-6022
402-333-8609
www.cccsn.org

Nevada

CCCS of Northern Nevada
575 East Plumb Lane, Suite 101
Reno, NV 89502
775-322-6557
www.fcsnv.org

Consumer Credit Counseling Service of Southern Nevada & Utah
2650 South Jones Boulevard
Las Vegas, NV 89146
702-364-0344
www.cccsnevada.org

New Hampshire

CCCS of New Hampshire & Vermont
105 Loudon Road, Building #1
Concord, NH 03301
603-224-6593
800-327-6778
www.cccsnh-vt.org
cccs@cccsnh-vt.org

CCCS – Portsmouth Northeast Credit Union
Money Management International
100 Borthwick Avenue
Portsmouth, NH 03802
866-889-9347
www.moneymanagement.org

New Jersey

CCCS of Central New Jersey (A Division of Family Guidance Center)
1931 Nottingham Way
Hamilton, NJ 08619
609-586-2574
888-379-0604
www.cccscentralnj.com

CCCS of New Jersey
185 Ridgedale
Cedar Knolls, NJ 07927
973-267-4324
888-726-3260
www.cccsnj.org

CCCS – South Jersey Branch
Money Management International
3073 English Creek Avenue, Suite 3
Egg Harbor Township, NJ 08234
866-889-9347
www.moneymanagement.org

CCCS – Tinton Falls Branch
Money Management International
106 Apple Street, Suite 105
Tinton Falls, NJ 07724
866-889-9347
www.moneymanagement.org

CCCS – Turnersville Plaza Office Center
Money Management International
5581 Route 42, Suite 6
Turnersville, NJ 08034
866-889-9347
www.moneymanagement.org

New Mexico

CCCS – Albuquerque Central Branch
Money Management International
2727 San Pedro NE, Suite 117
Albuquerque, NM 87110
866-889-9347
www.moneymanagement.org

CCCS – Albuquerque-Promenade Branch
Money Management International
5200 Eubank Boulevard, NE
Albuquerque, NM 87111
866-889-9347
www.moneymanagement.org

CCCS – Albuquerque-West Branch
Money Management International
3761 NM Highway 528
Albuquerque, NM 87114
866-889-9347
www.moneymanagement.org

CCCS – Farmington Branch
Money Management International
3001 Northridge Drive, Suite A
Farmington, MA 87401
866-889-9347
www.moneymanagement.org

CCCS – Las Cruces Branch
Money Management International
1065 South Main Street, Suite B-12
Las Cruces, NM 88005
866-889-9347
www.moneymanagement.org

CCCS – Santa Fe Branch
Money Management International
228 Saint Francis Drive, Suite C-2
Santa Fe, NM 87501
866-889-9347
www.moneymanagement.org

New York

CCCS – Bronx Branch
Money Management International
888 Grand Concourse, Suite 1K
Bronx, NY 10451
866-889-9347
www.moneymanagement.org

CCCS – Brooklyn Branch
Money Management International
26 Court Street, Suite 1801
Brooklyn, NY 11241
866-889-9347
www.moneymanagement.org

CCCS of Buffalo, Inc.
40 Gardenville Parkway, Suite 300
West Seneca, NY 14224
716-712-2060
www.cccsbuff.org

CCCS of Central New York, Inc.
500 South Salina Street, Suite 600
Syracuse, NY 13202-3394
315-474-6026
800-479-6026
www.credithelpny.org

CCCS – Manhattan Branch
Money Management International
11 Penn Plaza, Suite 5148
New York, NY 10001
866-889-9347
www.moneymanagement.org

CCCS – Queens Branch
Money Management International
88-32 Sutphin Boulevard, Third Room
Left
Jamaica, NY 11435
866-889-9347
www.moneymanagement.org

CCCS of Rochester, Inc.
50 Chestnut Plaza
Rochester, NY 14604
585-546-3440
888-724-2227
www.cccsroch.org

North Carolina

CCCS (A Division of Triangle Family Services)
401 Hillsborough Street
Raleigh, NC 27603
919-821-0790
800-283-6904
www.tfsnc.org

CCCS of the Carolina Foothills
200 Ohio Street
Spindale, NC 28160
828-286-7062
800-567-7062

CCCS of Catawba Valley
17 US Highway 70 SE
Hickory, NC 28602
828-322-1400
Web Site: www.fgcservices.com

CCCS of Fayetteville
316 Green Street
P.O. Box 2009
Fayetteville, NC 28302
910-323-3192
888-381-3720

CCCS of Forsyth County, Inc.
8064 North Point Boulevard
Suite 204
Winston-Salem, NC 27106
336-896-1191
888-474-8015
www.cccsforsyth.org

CCCS of Gaston County (A Division of Family Service, Inc.)
214 East Franklin Boulevard
Gastonia, NC 28052
704-862-0702
888-213-8853

CCCS of Greater Greensboro, a Division of Family Service of the Piedmont, Inc.
315 East Washington Street
Greensboro, NC 27401
336-373-8882
888-755-2227
www.thedebtdoc.com

CCS of Western North Carolina, Inc. d/b/a OnTrack Financial Education & Counseling

50 South French Broad Avenue
Suite 227
Asheville, NC 28801-3217
828-255-5166
800-737-5485
www.cccsofwnc.org

Consumer Credit Counseling Service

601 East 5th Street, Suite 400
Charlotte, NC 28202
704-332-9034
www.unitedfamilyservices.org

North Dakota

CCCS of the Village Family Service Center

1201-25th Street South
Fargo, ND 58103
701-235-3328
800-450-4019
www.thevillagefamily.org

Ohio

CCCS of Central Ohio, Inc.

4500 East Broad Street
Columbus, OH 43213
614-552-2222
800-355-2227
www.cccservices.com

CCCS of Lima

799 South Main Street
Lima, OH 45804
419-227-9202
www.consumercreditcounselingohio.org

CCCS of the Miami Valley (Sponsored By Graceworks Lutheran Services)

3131 South Dixie Drive, Suite 300
Dayton, OH 45439-2284
937-643-2227
www.cccsmv.org

CCCS of Portage County

143 Gougler Avenue
Kent, OH 44240
330-677-4124
www.portagefamilies.org

**LifeSpan Credit Counseling,
Consumer Credit Counseling Service**
1900 Fairgrove Avenue
Hamilton, OH 45011-1966
513-868-9220
888-597-2751
www.lifespanohio.org

Oklahoma

CCCS of Central Oklahoma, Inc.
3230 North Rockwell
Bethany, OK 73008-1789
405-789-2227
800-364-2227
www.cccsok.org

CCCS of Oklahoma, Inc.
4646 South Harvard
Tulsa, OK 74135
918-744-5611
800-324-5611
www.cccsofok.org

Oregon

**CCCS – Bend Branch
Money Management International**
1010 Northwest 14th Street, Suite 100
Bend, OR 97701
866-889-9347
www.moneymanagement.org

CCCS of Coos-Curry, Inc.
375 South 4th Street, Suite 100
Coos Bay, OR 97420
541-267-7040
www.cccscoos.org

**CCCS – Eugene Branch
Money Management International**
1200 High Street, Suite 150
Eugene, OR 97401
866-889-9347
www.moneymanagement.org

CCCS of Grants Pass
1314 Northeast Foster Way
Grants Pass, OR 97526
541-479-6002
Appointments: (541) 479-6002
www.cccsgrantspass.com

CCCS of Linn-Benton, Inc.
214 NW Hickory Street
Albany, OR 97321
541-926-5843
www.cccs-lb.org

CCCS of Mid-Willamette Valley, Inc.
1564 Commercial Street, SE
Salem, OR 97302
503-581-7301
888-254-8449
www.cccssalemoregon.com

CCCS of Southern Oregon, Inc.

820 Crater Lake Avenue, No. 202
Medford, OR 97504
541-779-2273
www.cccsso.org

Douglas CCCS

849 Southeast Mosher
Roseburg, OR 97470
541-673-3104
www.cccsdouglas.org

Pennsylvania

Advantage Credit Counseling Service, Inc.

River Park Commons
2403 Sidney Street, Suite 400
Pittsburgh, PA 15203
412-390-1300
888-511-2227
Web Site: www.cccspa.org

CCCS of Central Pennsylvania (A Division of Tabor Community Services, Inc.)

308 East King Street
Lancaster, PA 17602
717-397-5182
800-788-5062
www.cccscentralpa.org

CCCS of Delaware Valley

1515 Market Street, Suite 1325
Philadelphia, PA 19102
215-563-5665
800-989-2227
www.cccsdv.org

CCCS – Eastern Branch Money Management International

306 Spring Garden Street
Easton, PA 18042
866 889-9347
www.moneymanagement.org

CCCS of Northeastern Pennsylvania, Inc.

401 Laurel Street
Pittston, PA 18640
570-602-2227
800-922-9537
www.cccsnepa.org

CCCS – Pottstown Branch Money Management International

1954 East High Street
Pottstown, PA 19464
866-889-9347
www.moneymanagement.org

CCCS – Quakertown Branch
Money Management International
245 West Broad Street, Suite 3
Quakertown, PA 18951
866-889-9347
www.moneymanagement.org

CCCS – Whitehall Branch
Money Management International
3671 Cresent Court East
Whitehall, PA 18052
866-889-9347
www.moneymanagement.org

CCCS – Wyomissing Branch
Money Management International
833 North Park Road, Suite 103
Wyomissing, PA 18072
866-889-9347
www.moneymanagement.org

Rhode Island

CCCS – Providence Branch
Money Management International
4 Richmond Square, Suite 350
Providence, RI 02906
866-889-9347
www.moneymanagement.org

CCCS – Warwick Branch
Money Management International
501 Centerville Road
Warwick, RI 02886
866-889-9347
www.moneymanagement.org

South Carolina

CCCS/A Division of Compass of Carolina
1100 Rutherford Road
Greenville, SC 29609
864-467-3434
800-203-9692
www.compassofcarolina.org

Credit Counseling of Columbia,
A Program of Consumer Credit
Counseling Service
2712 Middleburg Drive, Suite 207-A
Columbia, SC 29204
803-733-5450
800-223-9213
Web Site: www.fsconline.org

Family Services CCCS
4925 LaCross Road, Suite 215
Charleston, SC 29406
843-744-1348
800-232-6489
www.familyserviceschassc.com

South Dakota

CCCS of the Black Hills
111 Saint Joseph Street
Rapid City, SD 57701
605-348-4550
800-568-6615
www.cccsbh.com

Consumer Credit Counseling Service of Lutheran Social Services of South Dakota
705 East 41st Street, Suite 100
Sioux Falls, SD 57105-6048
605-330-2700
888-258-2227
www.lsssd.org

Tennessee

CCCS – Kingsport Branch
Money Management International
1420 East Stone Drive
Kinsgport, TN 37664
866-889-9347
www.moneymanagement.org

Partnership for Families, Children and Adults, Inc./ CCCS Division
2245 A Olan Mills Drive
Chattanooga, TN 37421
423-490-5630
800-568-6615
www.partnershipfca.com

Texas

CCCS – Abilene Branch
Money Management International
500 Chestnut, Suite 1511
Abilene, TX 789602
866-889-9347
www.moneymanagement.org

CCCS – Beaumont Branch
Money Management International
5825 Phelan Boulevard, Suite 102
Beaumont, TX 77706
866-889-9347
www.moneymanagement.org

CCCS – Bedford Branch
Money Management International
4001 Airport Freeway, Suite 520
Bedford, TX 76021
866-889-9347
www.moneymanagement.org

CCCS – Burleson Branch
Money Management International
Huguley Professional Building
1161 Southwest Wilshire, Suite 116
Burleson, TX 76028
866-889-9347
www.moneymanagement.org

CCCS – Bryan/College Station
Branch
Money Management International
3833 South Texas Avenue, Suite 275
Bryan, TX 77802
866-889-9347
www.moneymanagement.org

CCCS – East Harris Co. Branch
Money Management International
12605 East Freeway, Suite 500
Houston, TX 77015
866-889-9347
www.moneymanagement.org

CCCS – Fort Hood Branch
Money Management International
761st Tank Battalion & Hood Road
Building 121, Room 126
Fort Hood, TX 76544
866-889-9347
www.moneymanagement.org

CCCS – Fort Worth Operations
Center
Money Management International
1320 South University Drive
Suite 200
Fort Worth, TX 76107
866-889-9347
www.moneymanagement.org

CCCS – Fuqua Branch
Money Management International
11550 Fuqua, Suite 350
Houston, TX 77034
866-889-9347
www.moneymanagement.org

CCCS of Greater Dallas, Inc.
8737 King George Drive, Suite 200
Dallas, TX 75235-2273
214-638-2227
800-249-2227
Web Site: www.cccs.net

CCCS of Greater San Antonio, Inc.
6851 Citizens Parkway, Suite 100
San Antonio, TX 78229
210-979-4300
www.cccssa.org

CCCS – Greenway Branch
Money Management International
One Greenway Plaza, Suite 130
Houston, TX 77046
866-889-9347

www.moneymanagement.org

CCCS – Humble Branch
Money Management International
125 West Main Street
Humble, TX 77338
866-889-9347

www.moneymanagement.org

CCCS – Killeen Branch
Money Management International
One Killeen Center
1711 East Central Texas Expressway #302
Killeen, TX 76541
866-889-9347

www.moneymanagement.org

CCCS – Lake Jackson Branch
Money Management International
122 West Way, Suite 407
Lake Jackson, TX 77566
866-889-9347

www.moneymanagement.org

CCCS – Lufkin Branch
Money Management International
2718-B South Medford Drive
Lufkin, TX 75901
866-889-9347

www.moneymanagement.org

CCCS – Mansfield Branch
Money Management International
1275 North Main Street, Suite 101-2
Mansfield, TX 76063
866-889-9347

www.moneymanagement.org

CCCS of North Central Texas, Inc.
901 North McDonald, Suite 600
McKinney, TX 75069
972-542-0257
800-856-0257

www.cccsnct.org

CCCS – Northeast Fort Worth Branch
Money Management International
1500 Corporate Circle, Suite 6
Southlake, TX 76092
866-889-9347

www.moneymanagement.org

CCCS – Northside Fort Worth Branch
Money Management International
The Vinnedge Building
2100 North Main Street, Suite 224
Fort Worth, TX 76106
866-889-9347
www.moneymanagement.org

CCCS – Odessa Branch
Money Management International
Ashford Park
2626 JBS Parkway, Suite B-103
Odessa, TX 79716
866-889-9347
www.moneymanagement.org

CCCS – Pyramid Plaza
Money Management International
3223 South Loop 289, Suite 416
Lubbock, TX 79423
866-889-9347
www.moneymanagement.org

CCCS – San Angelo Branch
Money Management International
3115 Loop 306, Suite 102
San Angelo, TX 76904
866-889-9347
www.moneymanagement.org

CCCS – Southeast Fort Worth Branch
Money Management International
Southeast YMCA Building
2801 Miller Avenue
Fort Worth, TX 76104
866-889-9347
www.moneymanagement.org

CCCS of South Texas
1706 South Padre Island Drive
Corpus Christi, TX 78416
361-854-4357
800-333-4357
www.cccsstx.org

CCCS – Spring/The Woodlands Branch
Money Management International
25025 I-45 North, Suite 525
The Woodlands, TX 77380
866-889-9347
www.moneymanagement.org

CCCS – Stafford Branch
Money Management International
12603 Southwest Freeway, Suite 625
Stafford, TX 77477
866-889-9347
www.moneymanagement.org

CCCS – Texas City Branch
Money Management International
Amegy Bank Building
2501 Palmer Highway, Suite 250
Texas City, TX 77590
866-889-9347
www.moneymanagement.org

CCCS – Waco Branch
Money Management International
6801 Sanger Avenue, Suite 202
Waco, TX 76710
866-889-9347
www.moneymanagement.org

CCCS – West Houston Branch
Money Management International
4600 Highway 6 North, Suite 250
Houston, TX 77084
866-889-9347
www.moneymanagement.org

CCCS – Whitney Bank Branch
Money Management International
1716 Mangum
Houston, TX 77092
866-889-9347
www.moneymanagement.org

CCCS – Willowbrook Branch
Money Management International
7915 FM 1960 West, Suite 240
Houston, TX 77070
866-889-9347
www.moneymanagement.org

CCCS of the YWCA/ Paso Del Norte Region
1600 Brown Street
El Paso, TX 79902
915-577-2530
888-533-7502
www.ywcaelpaso.org

Virginia

CCCS – Alexandria Branch
Money Management International
801 North Pitt Street, Suite 117
Alexandria, VA 22314
866-889-9347
www.moneymanagement.org

CCCS – Collinsville Branch
Money Management International
4846 Kings Mountain Road
Collinsville, VA 24078
866-889-9347
www.moneymanagement.org

CCCS – Fairfax Branch
Money Management International
3927 Old Lee Highway, Suite 101E
Fairfax, VA 22030
866-889-9347
www.moneymanagement.org

CCCS of Hampton Roads (A Program of Center for Child & Family Service, Inc.)
2021 Cunningham Avenue, Suite 400
Hampton, VA 23666
757-826-2227
www.debtfreeonline.com

CCCS – Leesburg Branch
Money Management International
604 South King Street, Suite 007
Leesburg, VA 20175
866-889-9347
www.moneymanagement.org

CCCS – Manassas Branch
Money Management International
10629 Crestwood Drive
Manassas, VA 20109
866-889-9347
www.moneymanagement.org

CCCS – Roanoke Branch
Money Management International
7000 Peters Creek Road
Roanoke, VA 24019
866-889-9347
www.moneymanagement.org

ClearPoint Financial Solutions, Inc.
8000 Franklin Farms Drive
Richmond, VA 23229
804-222-4660
877-877-1995
clearpointcreditcounselingsolutions.org

Washington

CCCS of Olympic-South Sound d/b/a Consumer Counseling Northwest
3560 Bridgeport Way West, Suite 1-D
University Place, WA 98466
253-588-1858
800-244-1183
www.ccnw.org

CCCS – Spokane Branch
Money Management International
4407 North Division, Suite 814
P.O. Box 5425
Spokane, WA 99207
866-889-9347
www.moneymanagement.org

CCCS of the Tri-Cities
401 North Morain
P.O. Box 6551
Kennewick, WA 99336
509-737-1973
800-201-2181
www.cccswaor.org

CCCS of Yakima Valley
1115 West Lincoln Avenue, Suite 119
Yakima, WA 98902
509-248-5270
800-273-6897
www.cccsyakima.org

West Virginia

CCCS of Huntington, a Division of Goodwill Industries
1102 Memorial Boulevard
Huntington, WV 25701
304-522-4321
888-534-4387
www.goodwillhunting.org

CCCS of the Mid-Ohio Valley
2715 Murdoch Avenue
B-4 Beechwood Plaza
Parkersburg, WV 26101
304-485-3141
866-481-4752
www.wvcccs.org

CCCS of North Central West Virginia (Criss-Cross, Inc.)
115 South 4th Street
P.O. Box 1831
Clarksburg, WV 26302
304-623-0921
800-498-6681
www.criss-crosswv.org

CCCS of Southern West Virginia
1219 Ohio Avenue
Dunbar, WV 25064
304-720-3640
800-281-5969
www.cccswv.com

Wisconsin

Catholic Charities Credit Counseling
3710 East Avenue South
La Crosse, WI 54601
608-782-0710
888-212-4357
www.cclse.org

CCCS of Beloit/Janesville
423 Bluff Street
Beloit, WI 53511
608-365-1244
www.cccsbeloit.com

CCCS of Greater Milwaukee

4915 South Howell Avenue, Suite 102
Milwaukee, WI 53207
414-482-8801
888-799-2227
www.creditcounselingwi.org

CCCS of Madison

128 East Olin Avenue, Suite 100
Madison, WI 53713
608-252-1320 x1134
www.fsmad.org

CCCS of Northeastern Wisconsin (FISC - A Program of Goodwill Industries)

1600 West 20th Street, Suite 140
Oshkosh, WI 54901
920-968-6346
800-366-8161
www.fisc-cccs.org

CCCS of Racine

420 Seventh Street
Racine, WI 53403
262-634-2391
www.fsracine.org

CCCS of Sheboygan (A Division of Family Service Association)

1930 North 8th Street, Suite 100
Sheboygan, WI 53081
920-458-3784
800-350-2227
www.cccsonline.org

Index

About the Authors

Wendell Schollander received his BA in economics and his MBA from the Wharton School of Finance at the University of Pennsylvania. He received his law degree from Duke University. Mr. Schollander has practiced law in the corporate and bankruptcy fields for more than thirty years. He has served as general counsel of RJR Archer and the Specialty Tobacco Counsel. Mr. Schollander currently practices law in Winston-Salem, North Carolina.

Wes Schollander received his BA from the University of North Carolina and his JD from Wake Forest School of Law. He is a member of the North Carolina Bar Association and the North Carolina Young Lawyers Association. Mr. Schollander currently practices law in Winston-Salem, North Carolina.